Levels 3–6

BREAKTHROUGH WRITING

David Grant

Julia Hubbard

Sarah Donnelly

Consultant: Cindy Torn

www.heinemann.co.uk

✓ Free online support
✓ Useful weblinks
✓ 24 hour online ordering

0845 630 44 44

Heinemann

Part of Pearson

Heinemann is an imprint of Pearson Education Limited, a company incorporated in England and Wales, having its registered office at Edinburgh Gate, Harlow, Essex, CM20 2JE. Registered company number: 872828

www.heinemann.co.uk

Heinemann is a registered trademark of Pearson Education Limited

Text © Pearson Education Limited 2009

First published 2009

13 12 11 10 09
10 9 8 7 6 5 4 3 2 1

British Library Cataloguing in Publication Data
A catalogue record for this book is available from the British Library.

ISBN 978 0 435806 24 8

Designed and produced by Wooden Ark
Original illustrations © Pearson Education 2009
Illustrated by Tony Forbes, Rory Walker, Paul McCaffrey, Kathryn Baker
Cover design by Wooden Ark
Picture research by Zooid Pictures
Cover photo/illustration © Getty Images
Printed in the United Kingdom by Scotprint

Acknowledgements
The author and publisher would like to thank the following individuals and organisations for permission to reproduce photographs:

: p26 WoodyStock/Alamy; : p36 Arvind Chenji/Alamy; p44 Helene Rogers/Art Directors & Trip Photo Library; p55 Andrew Paterson/Alamy; : p70 Photos 12/Alamy; p71 Moodboard/Corbis UK Ltd; p73 Stuart Kelly/Alamy; p76 (boys in canoe) Ariel Skelley/Corbis UK Ltd; p76 (boy abseiling) Strauss/Curtis/Corbis UK Ltd; p76 (tent in rain) Mark Phillips/Alamy; p76 (kids rafting) Alibi Productions/Alamy; p76 (beans on fire) Noel Hendrickson/Getty Images; : p90 The London Art Archive/Alamy; p94 Travelshots.com/Alamy; p97 Arnold Slater/Rex Features; : p106 Tony Watson/Alamy; p111 Trinity Mirror/Mirrorpix/Alamy; p114 Stephen Oliver/Alamy; :

p122 Pearson Education; p136 Ivan Cholakov/Shutterstock; p139 Alton Towers; : p147 Adrian Sherratt/Alamy; : p179 (gloves) Pearson Education; p179 (cake) Denise Kappa/Shutterstock; p179 (ketchup bottle) iStockphoto; p179 (roses) Filip Fuxa/Shutterstock; p179 (spade) iStockphoto; p179 (book) iStockphoto; p179 (ring) iStockphoto; p179 (wad of money) iStockphoto; p179 (cat) Eric Issel√©e/Shutterstock; p179 (key) Pearson Education; p179 (guitar) Elnur/Shutterstock; p180 (top) akg-images; p180 (bottom) Musée d'Orsay, Paris/Dagli Orti/Art Archive, p188 Janine Wiedel Photolibrary/Alamy; p195 Andrew Fox/Alamy; p201 Ken McKay/ Rex Features.

Every effort has been made to contact copyright holders of material reproduced in this book. Any omissions will be rectified in subsequent printings if notice is given to the publishers.

'The Salon Visit' from World's Shortest Stories by Steve Moss reprinted by permission of RP/Running Press, a member of Perseus Books Group; Here Lies Arthur Text Copyright Philip Reeve, 2007 Reproduced with permission of Scholastic Ltd All Rights Reserved; extract from Playing Dead by Tim Bowler, published by Oxford University Press, used with permission of David Higham Associates; Extract from Before I Die by Jenny Downham, published by David Fickling Books. Reprinted by permission of The Random House Group Ltd; Gatty's Tale by Kevin Cross-Holland reprinted by permission of Orion Children's Books, a division of The Orion Publishing Group, London; Leaflet, 'Your School, Your Say', used by permission of QCA Enterprises Ltd; Article 'Children's Rights? What about the rights of those who live in fear of young thugs?' by Melanie Phillips from the Daily Mail. Used by permission of the Daily Mail/Solo Syndication; Article 'Pupils plagiarise so much that we receive essays with adverts accidentally copied from internet, says teachers' by Sarah Harris from the Daily Mail. Used by permission of the Daily Mail/Solo Syndication; Article 'Fame Academy' by Dave Simpson from The Guardian. Used by permission of the Guardian News & Media; Reproduced with permission of Curtis Brown Group Ltd. London on behalf of William Boyd. Copyright© William Boyd 2006/Bloomsbury Publishers; Extract from Gordon Brown's Speech at the Labour Party Conference 2008, used by kind permission of the Labour Party; Extract from Winston Churchill is reproduced with permission of Curtis Brown Ltd, London on behalf of The Estate of Winston Churchill. Copyright © Winston Churchill; Extract from Winston Churchill is reproduced with permission of Curtis Brown Ltd, London on behalf of The Estate of Winston Churchill. Copyright © Winston Churchill; Extract from Somewhere Else by Sandra Glover. © Sandra Glover. Used by permission of Andersen Press Ltd; Article 'Gordon Brown's Labour Government Slash Tory poll lead' by Bob Roberts. Used by permission of the Mirror; Article 'Polls: Tories lead over Labour shrinks to single figures' by James Sturcke. Copyright Guardian News & Media Ltd 2008; Article 'Labour Closing Gap on Conservatives' by Rosa Prince; 'The Farmer's Wife' by Anonymous. Found in Anthology Axed Between The Ears Ed. David Kitchen; Extract from Beowulf translated by Seamus Heaney, published by Faber & Faber. Used by permission of the publisher.

Contents

CONTENTS

INTRODUCTION

Breakthrough Writing Levels 3 - 6 has been written to help you develop your writing skills in a flexible yet structured way which can be adapted to you and your learning.

This book contains two different sections: Skills and Practice. You can use the Skills section to develop your writing technique and then turn to the Practice pages to assess how far you have improved. Or you can use the Practice pages to test your skills, identifying the areas you need to work on, then use the Skills section to work on them.

The Skills section is divided into the eight Assessment Focuses which are not only the areas in which you will be assessed, but are also the key skills you need in order to achieve success in writing. Each Assessment Focus has been broken down into its component skills. In each of these, the book provides a series of structured activities to help you develop from Level 3 or 4, through Level 5, towards Level 6. At the end of each sequence of activities, there's a handy reminder of how the skills in each section progress from Level 3 to Level 6 so you can see how far you have come and what you need to do next.

Breakthrough has been written to improve your writing, so that you can see what you can already do, what you can improve on, and how to improve it. We hope you find it useful.

1.1 Planning

What am I learning?

You are learning how to plan and sequence your ideas.

Doing two things at the same time is much harder than doing one. If you don't plan a piece of writing, you will have to try to concentrate on **what you are going to write** at the same time as **how you are going to write it**. Planning before you write leaves your brain free to concentrate on choosing the best words and putting them in the best order.

Look at different ways to plan your writing.

 **ACTIVITY 1**

1 Look at these different writing plans. For each one, identify:

a one reason why you think it is an effective planning method – an **advantage**

b one reason why you think it is **not** an effective planning method – a **disadvantage**.

Map

Mother's cottage

Girl goes to visit Grandma

travels through woods

meets Wolf

arrives at Grandma's

Wolf has eaten Grandma and put on her clothes

a woodcutter hears cries and saves them

Spidergram

- Much healthier – 5 a day
- Environment: animals and global warming

Persuade: become vegetarian

- Slaughter – could you do it?
- Animals treated cruelly

Bulleted list

Year 9 Disco letter
- Tickets from Head of Year
- Professional DJ – amazing sound system and light show
- Food and drink available
- On Friday 18 July, 7 p.m. – 10 p.m.

Table

Review of *Mutant Netball Manager XII*

Good	Bad
Amazing graphics – looks great	Slow to play
Funny – characters and action	Too violent for younger players

Flowchart

| A man meets three witches. They predict he will become King. | Man kills the old king and becomes the new king. | Man keeps killing friends and rivals to stay as King. | People decide man must be stopped. They kill him. |

Sticky notes

Golden sand – kids making sandcastles – Dad buried up to neck

Packing up, cool breeze, sand between toes, walk up cliffs

Smell and sound of sea, fresh salt air and crashing waves

Blue sky, hot sun, gulls diving and swooping

Develop your plan to shape your writing.

1   There is no one planning method which suits every type of writing. You need to choose the best method **for you**, and **for the piece of writing** you are producing. Which of the planning methods on pages 6 and 7 would **you** choose if you were writing:

   a   a story
   b   an argument that your school sports facilities should be improved
   c   a letter persuading Year 9 students to enter a talent competition
   d   a factsheet to inform the reader about a famous person?

2   For each of your answers to question 1, write a sentence or two explaining your choice.

3   Once you have gathered your ideas, you need to decide on the best order or *sequence* in which to put them. You can sequence your ideas either by numbering them or by moving them around. Which of the planning methods shown on pages 6 and 7 are particularly good for letting you arrange and rearrange the sequence of your ideas?

4   Look at the plans which you identified in question 3. Choose **two** and decide on the best sequence in which to put the ideas.

Choose your best ideas.

1   Sometimes your *first* ideas aren't your *best* ideas. Look at the plan for this task:

> Persuade the person of your dreams to go out with you on Saturday night.

Persuade: Go out with me
- All my other boy/girlfriends said they liked going out with me.
- You can choose where we go and what we do.
- I promise you'll enjoy yourself.

   a   Think of three more ideas you could add to the plan.
   b   Which do you think are the **best four** points to use in writing the task? Write a sentence or two, explaining your choices.

Use your planning skills to prepare for writing.

1 a Choose **two** of the following tasks:

- A family of aliens knock on your front door. Describe them.
- Write a letter to the government persuading them to increase the length of school holidays.
- Write an article for a school newspaper to argue that computer games can be educational.
- Write a review of a favourite film, book or computer game.
- Write a leaflet informing parents about teenagers and how to deal with them.

Then for each one:

b Choose the best planning method for **you** and the **task**.

c Plan **six** points or ideas which you could use to complete the task, then choose the best **four**.

d Sequence your ideas in the best order.

e Write a few sentences to explain your decisions about:

- the planning method you chose
- the ideas you selected
- the sequence you chose to use.

IMPROVING YOUR LEVEL

Level 3	Level 4	Level 5	Level 6
Think about what you are going to write before you start writing	Choose the best planning method and use it to gather your ideas	Sequence your ideas to get them in the best order	Choose your best ideas, depending on the task, the purpose and the audience

REMEMBER

- **Identify** the best planning method for the writing task.
- **Gather** your ideas.
- **Choose** your best ideas.
- **Decide** on the sequence in which you will use your ideas.

1.2 Structuring a story

What am I learning?
You are learning how narrative fiction can be structured.

Imagine going on a holiday without planning it first. You get in the car and start driving with no idea of where you're going, how you're going to get there, or where you will stay when you arrive. Writing a story without planning it first has similar results: you go round in circles for a while without getting anywhere. Planning is an essential part of writing a story.

Look at a typical story structure.

Set-up
The situation at the start of the story.

↓

Conflict
A problem arises.

↓

Climax
The problem reaches a peak: how will things turn out?

↓

Resolution
The problem is sorted out, happily or sadly.

1 Almost every story – whether it's a fairy tale, a short story, a novel, play or film – can be summed up in four simple stages:

Look at the following examples.

Humpty Dumpty – **a nursery rhyme**

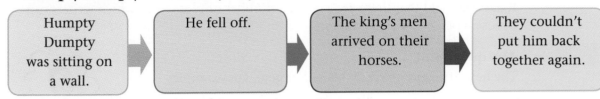

| Humpty Dumpty was sitting on a wall. | → | He fell off. | → | The king's men arrived on their horses. | → | They couldn't put him back together again. |

Romeo and Juliet by **William Shakespeare**

| Two families have been arguing and fighting for years. | → | A boy from one family and a girl from the other fall in love and marry in secret. | → | The boy commits murder and is sent away. The girl fakes her own death so she can be with him. | → | The boy commits murder and is sent away. The girl fakes her own death so she can be with him. |

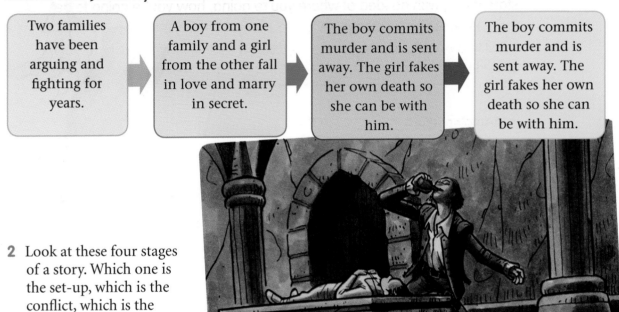

2 Look at these four stages of a story. Which one is the set-up, which is the conflict, which is the climax and which is the resolution?

A The boy discovers he is a wizard and goes to wizard school – where someone is trying to kill him.

B The boy and his friends find the magic stone and defeat the evil wizard.

C An orphan boy lives with relatives who treat him like a servant.

D The boy discovers that an evil and powerful wizard killed his parents and is trying to kill him – and will gain everlasting life and power if he finds a magic stone.

3 Think of a story you know well – it could be a fairy tale, a film or a novel. Write a short summary of the entire story, using the four stages of set-up, conflict, climax and resolution.

Develop your range of plot ideas.

It has been said that there are a limited number of plots from which writers can choose. Look at these examples.

The quest plot

The hero struggles to reach his or her goal. For example:

- A transformation quest

> CINDERELLA LONGS TO ESCAPE FROM HER STEPMOTHER AND SISTERS

- A treasure quest

> INDIANA JONES MUST OVERCOME THE ENEMY AND RECOVER THE LOST ARK

- A survival quest

> METEORITE ON COURSE TO COLLIDE WITH EARTH ... CAN THE HERO SAVE US?

The guest plot

Someone or something arrives and changes the characters' lives. For example:

- An uninvited guest

> THEY COULDN'T EXPLAIN THE STRANGE NOISES THEY HEARD AT NIGHT, UNTIL THEY REALISED THEY WERE NOT ALONE...

- An invited guest

> HE LOOKED SO ADORABLE AS A PUPPY. BUT THEN HE GREW UP ... AND UP!

The relationship plot

A story which focuses on the interaction of the characters. For example:

- Dangerous strangers

> ONE ACCIDENTAL MEETING
> WOULD CHANGE MACBETH'S
> LIFE ... FOREVER!

- Forbidden love

> SHE WASN'T ALLOWED TO SEE HIM – BUT
> SHE COULDN'T LIVE WITHOUT HIM

- Unfulfilled or lost love

> HE THOUGHT ABOUT HER EVERY MINUTE OF THE DAY
> – AND SHE DIDN'T EVEN KNOW HE EXISTED

Look again at the story you chose in your answer to question 3 on page 11. Does it fit any of the plots above? What kind of story is it?

Choose the best plot for your story.

ACTIVITY 3

1 a Look at these four story-writing tasks.

Write a story which begins with or includes this sentence:

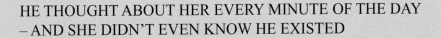

A She had no idea that moving to a new house would change her life so dramatically...

B It was the last thing he expected to find in his kitchen: a man slumped on the table...

C The moment she arrived, she knew that it was the strangest place she would ever see...

D Lying in the darkness, he heard a sound at the window. Someone was trying to get his attention...

b Which of the *genres,* or types, of story below could suit the story-writing tasks on page 13?

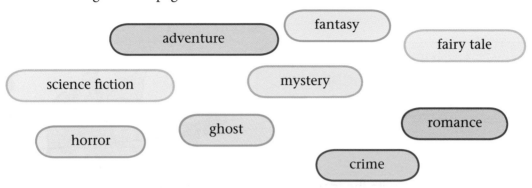

fantasy

adventure

fairy tale

science fiction

mystery

ghost

romance

horror

crime

c Look again at the story-writing tasks and the different genres you have matched with them. Which of these plot types could you use to help you write each story?

the quest plot

the relationship plot

the guest plot

Use a typical structure to plan a story.

 ACTIVITY 4

Using the four-part structure of set-up, conflict, climax and resolution, write a four-part plan for two of the story-writing tasks in Activity 3.

IMPROVING YOUR LEVEL

Level 3	Level 4	Level 5	Level 6
Write a story with a beginning, middle and end	Use the four part narrative structure: set-up, conflict-climax-resolution to plan your story	Use your knowledge of typical story structures to create your own original story	Consider the effect of genre and typical story structures when planning your story

REMEMBER

- **Set out** the four-part structure: set-up, conflict, climax, resolution.
- **Think** about the different kinds of plot you can choose from.
- **Plan** your story.

1.3 Experimenting with story structure

What am I learning?

You are learning how to manipulate narrative fiction structure to change the reader's response to your story.

Once you've come up with the idea for a story, you can develop your planning further by considering different ways in which you can organise or alter the events in the narrative. Writers may write and re-write and re-structure their plans several times before they choose the one which they think will be most effective.

Look at how a story can be structured.

1   Sometimes stories don't tell the whole story – the reader has to work out or *infer* some of the details or events. Read this very short story.

> **The Salon Visit**
> 'Anyway,' the woman in the chair continued, 'his wife's so *gullible!*
> Bill always says he's going bowling; she *always* believes him!'
> The beautician smiled. 'My husband William loves bowling.'
> *Never used to... Goes all the time now...*
> She paused, frowning.
> Then a slow, bitter smile emerged.
> 'Let's start on your perm. You're gonna look *unforgettable.*'

a   How many characters appear in the story?
b   How many characters actually **take part** in the story?
c   What does the beautician realise about half way through the story?
d   What does she decide to do about it?

2 Explain the story in just four sentences, using a table like the one below. Look back at page 10 if you need to remind yourself of this four part story structure.

Set-up	A woman tells her hairdresser that she is having an affair with a married man called Bill
Conflict	
Climax	
Resolution	

Develop your story ideas.

1 a The writer could have chosen to end the story differently. Which of these endings would you choose? The original ending:

'Let's start on your perm. You're gonna look *unforgettable.*'

Or something different?

The beautician put down her comb and picked up her largest scissors. 'I must be careful,' she smiled. 'These are *ever* so sharp.'

That night, the beautician went home with a bottle of peroxide bleach tucked in her handbag. 'Want a drink before you go bowling, William?' she said.

I'm going to burn his dinner on purpose, she thought to herself.

b Write a sentence or two explaining your answer to question 1a: the ending you chose and the ones you rejected.

2 Look at this plan for a story. Think of three different resolutions with which you could end the story.

Set-up: A husband and wife live a happy, simple life together in a small flat.

Conflict: One day, the husband finds a lottery ticket on the pavement. He takes it home and realises it's last night's winning ticket! He and his wife celebrate.

Climax: The husband wakes up the next morning. His wife has gone. And so has the lottery ticket.
Resolution: ?

Choose the best structure for the effect you want to create.

ACTIVITY 3

1 Look again at the story plan which you completed in Activity 2. Write it out on four separate pieces of paper or post-it notes.

Set-up: A husband and wife live a happy, simple life together in a small flat.

Climax: The husband wakes up the next morning. His wife has gone. And so has the lottery ticket.

Conflict: One day, the husband finds a lottery ticket on the pavement. He takes it home and realises it's last night's winning ticket! He and his wife celebrate.

Resolution: ?

2 Sometimes writers use *flashbacks* and *flashforwards* to change the order in which they tell the story. Reorganising the structure of a story can change the way a reader responds. Reorganise your story from Activity 3 for each sequence in A to D below. Which of the possible effects (1 to 4 below) do you think each new structure might have?

A Conflict – Set-up – Climax – Resolution

B Climax – Set-up – Conflict – Resolution

C Resolution – Set-up – Conflict – Climax

D Set-up – Conflict – Climax – Resolution

1 It grabs the reader's attention from the very start of the story.

3 It spoils the story because it gives away too much of the plot.

2 It increases the build-up of tension of the story.

4 It makes the reader want to find out more about the story.

Use a range of ideas and structures to experiment with story structure.

ACTIVITY 4

1 **a** Plan a simple story using the four-part structure. You can use some of the plot ideas on pages 12 and 13 to get you started.
 b Think of three different endings for your story. Choose the best one.
 c Experiment with the structure of your story. What happens if you start with the resolution and then flashback to the set-up? What is the effect if you start with the conflict, flashback to the set-up, then continue? Choose the most effective structure for your story.
 d Write two or three sentences explaining your choice of ending and structure.

IMPROVING YOUR LEVEL

Level 3	Level 4	Level 5	Level 6
Choose an appropriate ending for your story	Consider different endings to your story and choose the most effective	Select ideas for your story, considering their likely impact on the reader	Consider different ways in which you can structure your story and their likely impact on the reader

REMEMBER

- **Look** carefully at the four stages of your story.
- **Think** if any of the stages can be changed and improved, particularly the ending.
- **Explore** different ways in which you can organise the four parts of your story and the effect any changes will have.

1.4 Writing a character

What am I learning?

You are learning how writers create characters, narrators and their relationship with the reader.

A story cannot live without characters. They are the people whose stories the writer must make us want to find out about; the people who need to hold our attention for as long as the story lasts.

Look at how writers create characters.

ACTIVITY 1

1　Read this extract taken from the opening chapter of *Here Lies Arthur* by Philip Reeve, a retelling of the famous story of King Arthur and his knights.

> **byre:** cowshed
>
> **Artorius Magnus:** Arthur the Great
>
> **Dux Bellorum:** the leader of battles

Even the woods are burning. I plunge past the torched **byre** and hard into the shoulder-deep growth of brambles between the trees, but there's fire ahead of me as well as behind. The hall on the hill's top where I thought I'd find shelter is already blazing. I can hear men's voices baying like hounds on a scent, the hooves of horses on the winter earth like drums. I see their shadows long before the riders themselves come in sight. Fingers of darkness stretch from their raggedy banners, reaching through the smoke which hangs beneath the trees. I duck sideways into a brambled hollow and wriggle deep. Thorns tug at my dress and snag my hair. The ground's frosty. Hard and cold under my knees and fingers. Fear drags little noises out of me. I squeak and whimper like a hunted cub.

But it's not me these horsemen are hunting. I'm nothing to them. Just a lost girl-child scurrying across the corners of their war. They thunder past without seeing me, the firelight bright on spears and swords, on mail and burnished helmets, on shield bosses and harness buckles and fierce faces lit up like lanterns. Their leader's out in front on a white horse. Big, he is. Shiny as a fish in his coat of silver scales. The cheek-guards of his helmet ripple with fire-gleam and his teeth between them are gleaming too, bared in a hard shout.

You've heard of him. Everyone's heard of Arthur. **Artorius Magnus**; the Bear; the **Dux Bellorum**; the King that Was and Will Be. But you haven't heard the truth. Not till now. I knew him, see. Saw him, smelled him, heard him talk. When I was a boy I rode with Arthur's band all up and down the world, and I was there at the roots and beginnings of all the stories.

2 Do you think the writer has succeeded in interesting the reader in his narrator?

3 Writers can tell us about characters by describing who they are, what they say, what they do, and how they look. What did you discover about the narrator in this extract? Remember that because this character is the narrator, she 'says' every word in the story.

Use a table like the one below to record your answers.

Who the character is	
What the character says	
What the character does	
How the character looks	

Develop ways to describe a character.

1 Look again at the four ways in which a writer can tell the reader about a character. What does the writer **not** tell us about the character of the narrator in the extract on page 19?

2 Choose what you think are the **two** most effective ways to create a character. Use them to plan a character from a story. You can choose one of those below, or think of your own.

- The nastiest student in the school
- The Year 7 student on their first day at secondary school
- The grumpy old man/woman
- Your favourite aunt/uncle

Choose from a range of techniques to create an effective character.

1 Some stories are written in the **first person**, others are written in the **third person**.

Here Lies Arthur is written in the first person. Look at this extract. It is the first paragraph of the novel, rewritten in the third person:

> **first person:** the narrator telling the story is a character within the story, referring to themselves as 'I'
>
> **third person:** the narrator is not a character within the story and refers to the characters as *he* or *she*

> Even the woods are burning. She plunges past the torched byre and hard into the shoulder-deep growth of brambles between the trees, but there's fire ahead of her as well as behind. The hall on the hill's top where she thought she'd find shelter is already blazing. She can hear men's voices baying like hounds on a scent, the hooves of horses on the winter earth like drums. She sees their shadows long before the riders themselves come in sight.

Has changing this extract to the third person changed the effect of the story in any way? Why do you think the writer chose to write the story in the first person?

2 One effect of writing in the first person is to create a closer relationship with the reader. The writer of *Here Lies Arthur* has added to this effect: the narrator talks directly to the reader, using the word 'you'.

   a What does the narrator tell the reader when she is talking directly to them?
   b What does this suggest about the narrator?
   c What effect is this intended to have on the reader?

Use a range of techniques to create an effective character.

Write the opening few lines of a story in which you introduce the main character you planned in Activity 2. Aim to make the reader want to read on, to find out what you're going to tell them. Decide whether you will:

- describe who they are, what they say, what they do, how they look
- write in the first person
- talk directly to the reader.

IMPROVING YOUR LEVEL

Level 3	Level 4	Level 5	Level 6
Give some basic details about a character	Develop the details you use to describe your character, eg their appearance	Develop your character in more detail, describing their appearance, what they say and do	Consider the way in which you will present your character(s), considering their likely impact on the reader

REMEMBER

- **Think** about the different ways in which you can create a character.
- **Decide** whether you will write in the first or third person.
- **Use** your character to make the reader want to read on, using tricks such as promising them information or addressing them directly.

1.5 Character-building

What am I learning?

You are learning how to use a range of techniques for building an effective character.

Writers use a range of techniques to develop interesting characters, choosing their voice and personality according to the effect they want to create.

Look at how one writer builds a character.

1 Read this extract taken from the opening of Tim Bowler's novel, *Blade: Playing Dead.* The narrator, known as Blade, is in a police station, talking to a police officer – Blade refers to him as 'Pugface' – following an incident in which Blade stood on a zebra crossing for several minutes, obstructing traffic and abusing drivers. A policewoman is also present.

'The driver's told us he doesn't wish to take things further. He just wanted to report the incident.'
Say nothing.
   'He was a bit worried we might not be able to trace the boy who held up the traffic for five minutes, swore at all the drivers, then ran off.' Pugface sniffs. 'He clearly wasn't aware just how well we know you round here.'
   He leans closer. I'm hating this now. It's not the police station. It's this face leering down at me. He's got to pull back. He's got to do it now, right now.
   But he doesn't. He just smirks again—then leans even closer.
   'Do you really think,' he whispers, 'that we haven't noticed you've got something hidden inside your sock?'
   I lunge for the knife—in vain. The man's hands are tight round my arms. I don't even see the woman move. One minute she's over by the door, the next she's behind me, pulling me back against the chair. I spit at 'em, snarl at 'em, try to break free. Doesn't do any good…

The woman pulls out the knife, fumbles with the other sock.

'There's nothing in there,' I yell.

She checks anyway, then straightens up, holding the knife. The man lets go of me and takes it from her. I duck under their arms and make a dash for the door.

I'm not fast—no point pretending—but being small sometimes helps, and somehow I've taken 'em by surprise. I'm at the door before 'em. I can see Pugface's hands clutching at me, and the woman's, but they're kind of falling over each other.

Then I'm out in the corridor.

Shouts from inside the room. Some constable running towards me from the desk. That's when fire extinguishers come in handy. A squirt over the guy and he slips. Jump over him and out the door.

Nothing to it.

And that was when I was seven.

Now that I've turned fourteen, I look back and you know what's weird? It's like nothing's changed. I still don't like the police and I still don't like people getting close.

And that includes you, Bigeyes.

2 a What are your first impressions of the character of Blade? Write down three words to describe him.

 b For each of your answers, write down a piece of evidence from the extract.

Develop techniques for building a character.

ACTIVITY 2

1 a Look at these two different versions of the same incident from the extract:

The original version in which we are **shown** what Blade is like:

A

One minute she's over by the door, the next she's behind me, pulling me back against the chair. I spit at 'em, snarl at 'em, try to break free.

A different rewritten version in which we are **told** what Blade is like:

B

When the police grabbed hold of him, Blade tried to break free. He was an aggressive boy who wasn't afraid of the police.

Which version is more effective in building the character of Blade and holding the reader's attention? Why?

c For each of your answers to question 2b on page 24, decide whether the writer **told** you **directly** what Blade is like, or whether he told you **indirectly** by **showing** you what Blade says and does.

2 Imagine the characters of three different 14-year-old girls. Thinking about **what they say** and **what they do**, write down as many different ways as you can to **show** that they are:

Characteristics	What she says	What she does
a kind and generous		
b angry		
c a liar		

Choose a range of techniques for building a character.

 **ACTIVITY 3**

1 a What surprise does the writer of *Blade* reveal at the end of the extract on pages 23 and 24?
   b How does this *contrast* with the way the writer has described the character of Blade in the rest of the extract?
   c What effect does this have on the reader?

2 One way of creating an engaging story is to use *contrast*, either by placing an ordinary person in an extraordinary situation – or by placing an extraordinary person in an ordinary situation. Which contrasting combination of the following characters, personalities and situations would create the most engaging story, do you think?

Character	Aged	Who is...	Situation
A soldier	30	loud and aggressive	fighting in a war
A boy	9	quiet and hard working	going to school
A businesswoman	64	greedy and selfish	running a large company

3 a Look at the way in which Blade speaks – both to the other characters and as a narrator. Which of these techniques does the writer use to create his voice?

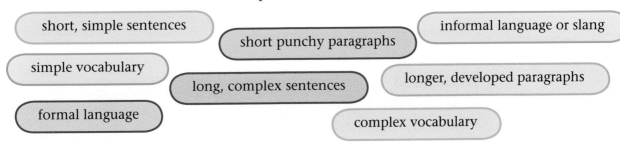

short, simple sentences

short punchy paragraphs

informal language or slang

simple vocabulary

long, complex sentences

longer, developed paragraphs

formal language

complex vocabulary

   b Look again at the character you selected in question 2. Which of the above techniques would you use to create their 'voice'?

Use a range of different techniques to build a character.

You are lost in a forest. You see a dark, rundown house in a clearing. You knock on the door. Plan two characters: a narrator knocking on the door, and the person who answers. Remember to think about:

- *showing* the reader what your characters are like, not telling them
- using contrast in your characters
- creating contrast between character and situation
- techniques to create an appropriate voice for the narrator.

IMPROVING YOUR LEVEL

Level 3	Level 4	Level 5	Level 6
Give some basic details about a character	Tell the reader what the character is like, eg selfish, friendly	Try to show the reader what the character is like using their dialogue and actions	Use the way your character speaks to show the reader more about them

REMEMBER

- Don't *tell* your reader what your characters are like – *show* them.
- Use contrast to surprise and engage your reader.
- Use a range of techniques to create an appropriate voice for your characters.

1.6 Creating setting and atmosphere

What am I learning?

You are learning how writers select details to create an effective setting in a story.

As a writer, you need to descibe the *setting* of your story as well as your characters, not only so that your reader knows where the story happens, but also to help create the right mood or atmosphere for the story.

Look at how writers create different settings and atmospheres.

ACTIVITY 1

1   Read these extracts, taken from the openings of two novels.

Text A is taken from the opening of *Before I Die* by Jenny Downham.

A

I can smell sausages. Saturday night is always sausages. There'll be mash and cabbage and onion gravy too. Dad'll have the lottery ticket and Cal will have chosen the numbers and they'll sit in front of the TV and eat dinner from trays on their laps. They'll watch *The X Factor*, then they'll watch *Who Wants to Be a Millionaire?* After that, Cal will have a bath and go to bed and Dad'll drink beer and smoke until it's late enough for him to sleep.

He came up to see me earlier. He walked over to the window and opened the curtains. 'Look at that!' he said as light flooded the room. There was the afternoon, the tops of the trees, the sky. He stood silhouetted against the window, his hands on his hips. He looked like a Power Ranger.

Text B is taken from the opening of *Gatty's Tale* by Kevin Crossley-Holland.

B

In one corner of the cow-stall, the heap of dirty sacking shifted. Something buried beneath it made a sound that began as a gentle murmur and ended as a grouse.

Then the cock crowed and that loosed the tongues of his disciples. Half the neighers and brayers and bleaters and grunters in the manor of Caldicot welcomed the day's dawning, chill and misty as it was.

As soon as Hopeless joined in and mooed, the heap of sacking shrugged and then tossed. In one fluid movement, Gatty stood up, crossed herself, reached for her russet woollen tunic lying on a bale of hay, and pulled it on over her undershirt and baggy drawers…

'Greetings in God!' she said politely to her cow. She gave Hopeless a handful of grain, pulled up her three-legged stool, and began to milk her.

2 How would you describe these two settings? Write a sentence to describe each one.

3 In these extracts the writers select and describe details to create different settings. Use a table like the one below to identify how the writer selects details to give the reader a sense of time, place and mood.

	Text A	Text B
Time		
Place		
Mood		

Develop ways of creating setting and atmosphere.

1 There are only five ways in which human beings can take in information about the world around them: the five senses of sight, sound, smell, touch and taste. Writers can use these to tell readers what it would be like to be wherever the story is taking place, experiencing it with their own five senses.

Which of the five senses do the writers of Texts A and B on page 27 use to describe the setting of their story? Write down a quotation for each example you identify.

2 Plan the opening of a story in which you describe yourself standing in a busy school playground. Use a table like this:

Sight	
Sound	
Smell	
Touch	
Taste	

Choose descriptive details to build an effective atmosphere.

1 As well as describing the setting, writers aim to create a mood or atmosphere which will add to their story. They can do this by choosing:

- the kind of location in which the story is set
- the weather
- the time of day.

Imagine you have been asked to complete one of the following writing tasks.

Write a story about one of your happiest memories.

Write a story about a time when you were frightened.

a In what kind of location would you set each story? For example, if you decided to set it in a house, what *kind* of house would you choose to describe? If you decided to set it in a forest, what *kind* of forest?

b What kind of weather would you choose for each story? Sunshine and blue sky? Or clouds and thunder?

c At what time of day would you set the main events of your story? Lunchtime? Or the middle of the night?

2 To set a scene effectively, writers do not describe every detail of a scene – they choose those details which will create an atmosphere to suit their story.

Look at the pictures below.

Choose just **three** details from each picture which you think will give the reader a good idea of the setting and its atmosphere. Write a sentence describing each detail you choose.

Use a range of techniques to create an effective setting and atmosphere.

 ACTIVITY 4

1 You are writing a story about a day on which something amazing happened in your house. Write the opening paragraph of the story, creating an ordinary, everyday atmosphere which will contrast with this surprising event.

2 You are writing a story about the time when you worked as a spy. You have woken up in a hotel room. You immediately realise that something is wrong. Write the opening paragraph of the story creating a tense, exciting atmosphere.

IMPROVING YOUR LEVEL

Level 3	Level 4	Level 5	Level 6
Tell the reader where your story is set	Tell the reader what the setting of your story looks like	Use the five senses to describe the setting of your story	Choose descriptive details to suggest the mood or atmosphere of your setting, eg time, weather, senses etc

REMEMBER

- **Use** the five senses to describe the setting of your story.
- **Choose** and describe the *kind* of location, the time and the weather.
- **Select** just a few details which will help create an appropriate and effective atmosphere.

AF1 Sample Answers: Levels 3–6

IMAGINE

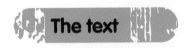

The text

A security guard is on duty at Farnstead Manor, the stately home of Lord and Lady Farnstead-Barnsworth. His job is to protect a valuable diamond which Lord Farnstead-Barnsworth is trying to sell. However, there are rumours that The Cat – the world famous jewel thief – is about to commit the most daring robbery of his career and help himself to the precious jewel...

The question

1 Identify the key words in the question.

2 Identify the Assessment Focus which the question is assessing.

Write the opening of this story, aiming to:
- engage the reader's attention and interest
- describe the setting
- create an appropriate mood or atmosphere
- introduce one of the characters.

Writing Assessment Focus 1:

Write imaginative, interesting and thoughtful texts by:
- choosing imaginative and relevant details
- structuring your writing to create an effect on the reader
- using a range of techniques.

31

Level 3

- I sometimes choose good, imaginative ideas.
- I try to choose words to describe the characters and the setting.
- Sometimes I can write as if I am a character in a story – but sometimes I start writing as if I am me again.

> I am called Lord Farnstead-Barnsworth and I have a very valuable diamond. I am worried that a robber is going to steal my diamond so I have got a security guard who looks after it all day and all night.
>
> Well, one night I was sleeping in bed when I heard a terrible crash from downstairs. I went downstairs and it was very dark. There was a man with a torch creeping around.
> 'What are you doing here?' said Lord Farnstead-Barnsworth.

Although this tells the story clearly, it is not written with descriptive detail or structured to grab the reader's attention.

Good attempt at building up tension.

Begins in the first person, writing as Lord Farnstead-Barnsworth but moves into the third person here.

Some selection of detail and description.

Level 4

- I usually plan and choose good, imaginative ideas.
- I usually describe the characters and the setting.
- I usually write from the same point of view throughout a piece of writing.

> I heard a rustling noise from the garden. It sounded like someone moving through the bushes. I went out the front door and shone my torch around. There was something in the shadows.
>
> I turned off my torch and walked slowly and silently into the garden. The moon was shining but it disappeared behind a cloud. That was when I felt a thump on the back of my head. When I woke up it was morning and the diamond was gone.

Written from an imaginative and consistent point of view.

Some effective choice of detail and description.

Some missed opportunities for description of the setting and the action.

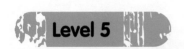

Level 5

- I plan and choose good, imaginative ideas, developing them in more detail before I start writing.
- I describe the characters and setting in detail.
- I sometimes choose the point of view and 'voice' in which I will write a story and usually stay 'in role'.

> My husband Lord Farnstead-Barnsworth stood in <u>his stripy pyjamas and dressing gown with his mouth open.</u>
>   '<u>It's been nicked!'</u> he said.
>   '<u>First you decide to sell my diamond,'</u> I shouted. '<u>And now you've lost it, you stupid man! I wish I'd never married you! My mother gave me that diamond!'</u>
>   '<u>It's his fault,'</u> said my husband, pointing at the <u>fat, red-faced security guard.</u> 'He was supposed to be looking after it.'

Imaginative ideas and choice of narrator.

Good use of dialogue to develop story and character.

Effective choice of detail and description.

Inconsistent choice of language, perhaps.

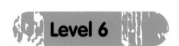

Level 6

- I choose the best way to plan and structure my writing, and the details which I will focus on, depending on the task.
- I can use a range of different techniques to create effective characters and settings.
- I usually choose the point of view and 'voice' in which I will write a story and maintain it throughout.

> <u>I climbed through the window of Farnstead Manor and froze.</u> <u>All I could hear was the creaking of a pair of shoes. No, they were boots. Size 9, black leather. Steel toe caps.</u>
>   Ahead of me the beam of a torch shone around the corridor as if looking for something. It shone on <u>the polished wooden floor and the oil paintings on the wall</u> but it did not shine on me. I was too quick. <u>It takes more than a torch to catch The Cat!</u>
>   <u>I paused by a mirror to check my hair and makeup in the moonlight and went on my way to the safe in which Lord Farnstead-Barnsworth kept his precious diamond, soon to be mine.</u>

Well planned focus highlighting a moment of tension in the story.

Very imaginative and surprising choice of descriptive detail, clearly selected for effect: to develop character and humour.

Effective choice of detail and description.

Choice of descriptive detail builds a picture of setting for the reader.

AF2 PURPOSE, AUDIENCE AND FORM

2.1 What's the question?

What am I learning?

You are learning to read a writing task and identify the purpose, audience and form required.

Before you start any piece of writing, you need to be aware of its purpose, the audience you are writing for, and the form in which you need to write. If you can work this out before you start planning and writing, you are much more likely to produce a text which meets the requirements of the task.

Look at a range of writing tasks.

Read through these writing tasks.

> **A** You are a journalist for a local newspaper. You have received this email from your editor.
>
> From: the Editor
> Subject: Front page news
> The teenager who won that TV talent show is coming home today.
> I want you to get to his house at 32 Billings Road, find out all about
> him and write a report for the front page. Make sure you get all
> the details of the competition and comments from all the relevant
> people – him, his parents, his neighbours and friends.
>
> **Write the front page report, informing readers about the teenager's arrival back in his home town.**
> You should include a headline, but not set your report out in columns.

B The Head of Year 7 is producing pages for the school website to help new Year 7 students settle into your school. She wants a web page which gives the students' point of view. She has asked for your help.

Write a contribution for the website, advising new Year 7 students what to expect and how to make the most of life at your school.

C Your head teacher has announced that your school is very short of money this year and so all after-school activities have been cancelled.

Write a letter persuading your head teacher to change his or her mind.

D **Write a review of a favourite book, film or computer game for a teenage magazine.**

E New research suggests that children learn much more in the morning. Your school has decided to change the school day so it starts at 7 a.m. and finishes at lunchtime.

Write an article for your school newspaper arguing against this idea.

F

Competition

Your local tourist information centre wants to attract more visitors to your area, so they're inviting local residents to write a leaflet informing visitors about all the different things there are to see and do. The best entry will win a year's free visits to the cinema, swimming pool and bowling alley – so get writing!

Write the text for the leaflet.

Develop your awareness of audience, purpose and form.

ACTIVITY 2

1 Usually, writing tasks clearly state the purpose and form. For example:

> **Write a letter persuading your head teacher to change his or her mind.**

For each of the writing tasks on pages 34 and 35:

a Identify the **purpose** for which you are being asked to write, and the **form** which you should use.

b Write down the **key words** which gave you this information.

Use the purpose and form banks below to help you.

The purpose bank *The reason for writing*		The form bank *The format and context of the writing*
argue	inform	newspaper article
persuade	explain	magazine article
advise	describe	letter
analyse	imagine/entertain	leaflet
review		web page

2 The audience for a text can usually be described by its age and gender. For example:

Age	Gender
children	men
teenagers	women
young adults	men and women
middle-aged adults	
retired people	

Writing tasks often tell you the audience you are aiming at. Look again at the writing tasks in Activity 1. For each of them:

a Identify the **audience** for which you are being asked to write.

b Write down the **key words** which gave you this information.

Choose an appropriate purpose and audience.

 **ACTIVITY 3**

1 Sometimes, you may need to think more carefully about the purpose and the audience you will aim at: you need to 'read between the lines'. Look at the task below, for example.

A new theme park is opening in your area. It will offer:
- rides to suit everyone, from 3-year-olds to 93-year-olds
- a soft play area for toddlers
- a café serving delicious snacks and meals
- family value tickets for two adults and up to three children.

Write the text for a leaflet advertising the theme park.

a What is the **purpose** of advertising?
b Although the theme park has been designed for families, who is likely to make the decision to visit the park?
c What are the **purpose** and **audience** for this writing task?

Use your reading skills to identify a task's purpose, audience and form.

 **ACTIVITY 4**

1 For each of these tasks, write down the purpose, audience and form required, and the key words which gave you this information.

a Write a leaflet advising school students how to achieve the best results in English exams.
b Write a magazine article advising how to keep young children fit and healthy.
c You are the first person to set foot on the planet Mars. Write a letter to an astronaut friend, telling them all about your trip so they will want to come with you next time.

IMPROVING YOUR LEVEL

Level 3	Level 4	Level 5	Level 6
Identify the purpose and form specified in a writing task	Identify the purpose and form specified in a writing task	Identify the purpose, audience and form specified in a writing task	Be aware of the purpose and audience for which you are writing, even when unspecified in the task

REMEMBER

- **Read** the question carefully.
- **Identify** the purpose, audience and form using the key words in the task.
- **Read** 'between the lines' if the task does not clearly tell you the purpose or audience for which you are writing.

2.2 Writing for purpose and audience

What am I learning?

You are learning how to structure and shape your writing for specific purposes and audiences.

Every type of writing has a range of key features which will help you make sure your writing achieves its purpose. If you use these to plan your work, you can then concentrate on writing with your audience in mind.

Look at the key features of a range of writing purposes.

ACTIVITY 1

Write to argue

Aim: to present the writer's opinion

Effect: to influence the reader's opinion

Structure: makes a series of points

Paragraphs: each point supported by evidence and an explanation

Language: usually formal, depending on the audience

Special features: often makes use of *rhetorical devices* such as questions, emotive language

Write to persuade

Aim: to present the writer's opinion

Effect: to influence the reader's actions or attitudes

Structure: makes a series of points

Paragraphs: each point supported by evidence and an explanation

Language: usually formal, depending on the audience

Special features: often makes use of *rhetorical devices* such as questions, emotive language

Write to advise

Aim: to give advice

Effect: to help the reader solve a problem

Structure: makes a series of suggestions

Paragraphs: each suggestion supported by evidence and an explanation

Language: depends very much on the audience

Special features: often makes use of *modal verbs* (You should... You must... You could...) and *commands* (Don't... Remember..., etc.)

Write to explain

Aim: to tell the reader *how* or *why*

Effect: to help the reader understand or achieve something

Structure: a series of key points

Paragraphs: a topic sentence on which further sentences expand

Language: depends very much on the audience

Special features: often uses personal experience to illustrate the explanation

Write to describe

Aim: to create a picture with words

Effect: to transfer that picture to the reader

Structure: a series of key features

Paragraphs: a topic sentence on which further sentences expand

Language: depends very much on the audience

Special features: varied vocabulary, focusing on the five senses: sight, sound, smell, touch and taste

Write to inform

Aim: to present facts clearly

Effect: to give the reader information

Structure: a series of key points or features

Paragraphs: a topic sentence on which further sentences expand

Language: depends very much on the audience

Special features: often organised using bullet points or subheadings

Write to analyse

Aim: to present a balanced view on an idea, a situation, a text, etc.

Effect: to explore ideas and sometimes help the reader come to their own conclusion

Structure: a series of points

Paragraphs: each point supported by evidence and an explanation

Language: usually formal

Special features: usually written in the third person to suggest an objective point of view

Write to review

Aim: to give the pros and cons

Effect: to help the reader choose what to buy, where to go, etc.

Structure: may present all the pros then the cons, or alternate them

Paragraphs: each point supported by evidence and an explanation

Language: often less formal, depending on the audience

Special features: often uses exaggeration to emphasise the good and bad features

Write to imagine and entertain

Aim: usually to tell a story

Effect: to amuse or inspire the reader

Structure: usually gives a set-up (the situation in which the story takes place), then a problem arises which is resolved

Paragraphs: may be description using topic sentences on which further sentences expand – or dialogue

Language: depends very much on the audience

Special features: key features are much more flexible!

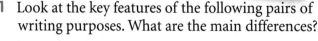

1 Look at the key features of the following pairs of writing purposes. What are the main differences?

   a **argue** and **persuade**

   b **analyse** and **review**

   c **describe** and **imagine/entertain**

Develop your awareness of register.

1 Look at this text.

   a Who do you think is the intended audience for this text?
   b How can you tell? Is it the topic of the writing? Or the writer's choice of language?

4 In the same way that you need to choose the right level of difficulty for the language in your writing, you also need to think about the level of formality, or *register*: formal or informal

   a There are lots of ways of greeting someone. Rank the greetings below in order of formality.

Fred cannot see Freda. She is hiding. He calls to her. Fred stays very still.

(Hello)　(Alright?)　(Good morning)　(How you doing?)　(Hiya)

   b Choose three different ways of greeting someone. For each one, write down a situation in which it would be appropriate to use it.

3 Look at these two writing tasks:

   • Write an information sheet for new teachers at your school.
   • Write an information sheet for new students at your school.

   a Which of the two tasks is more likely to contain formal language?
   b Look at extracts A and B below. From which of the two tasks above do you think they have been taken?

   A The school canteen serves hot meals and sandwiches between 12.30 and 1.15 p.m. Students must queue. However, staff are permitted to go straight to the counter.

   B When the bell for lunch goes, leggit to the canteen or you'll be stuck in a queue for hours.

   c Identify examples of formal and informal language which helped you work out the intended audience for each extract.

Choose your register for effect.

1 Look at these two extracts from a student's piece of writing to analyse. They are looking at the effects of global warming.

A

It is widely believed that, as a result of human activity, carbon dioxide is building up in the earth's atmosphere and the temperature of the planet is rising.

B

Don't bin it – recycle it!

    a How would you describe the *register* of the two different extracts?

    b What two different effects is the writer hoping their choice of register will have on the reader?

Use your awareness of audience and purpose to select an appropriate register.

1 The end-of-term school disco is due to take place in six weeks' time. You need to persuade:

- students to buy tickets
- teachers to supervise the event.

    a Write two short articles for your school newspaper, one aimed at students, and one aimed at teachers. Remember to use an appropriate register. Try to vary your register for effect.

    b Write two or three sentences explaining the decisions you made in your writing.

IMPROVING YOUR LEVEL

Level 3	Level 4	Level 5	Level 6
Understand the difference between different writing purposes	Show some awareness of your audience when choosing the style of your writing	Select language which is consistently appropriate in complexity and register for your audience	Select the register of your writing, considering its likely effect on your reader

REMEMBER

- Identify the key features of the writing purpose.
- Select an appropriate register for your purpose and audience.
- Consider using a different register for effect.

2.3 Selecting and presenting your points

What am I learning?

You are learning how to select from a range of points depending on your audience.

When you are writing for a specific audience, you need to think about the *register* in which you will write, choosing language which is appropriate to your reader and your purpose. However, you also need to think about the material you select, and the points that you will choose, depending on the audience for your writing.

Look at the details.

ACTIVITY 1

The notes below and on the following page were made by a student who was asked to write an article for the student newspaper about the end-of-term disco.

<u>End-of-term disco</u>
- Started at 7.00 p.m. in the hall
- Not many people at start – just Suni and Jo (from school council – they organised it all) and a bunch of teachers hanging around chatting
- Suni said they'd sold 107 tickets
- Ben was the DJ
- Ben used his dad's equipment (he does a local mobile disco called Gold Star Disco)
- The lights were really good – and a smoke machine!
- Micah and Kayleigh on refreshments – watery orange squash and cheap biscuits
- 7.30 people started turning up
- 8.00 really crowded – everyone standing round the room, keeping off the dance floor

- 8.30 people finally started dancing – couldn't move on the dance floor – bit sweaty and smelly!!
- 9.00 some Year 11s turned up, hanging around outside and making trouble, Boggy and Dan and Natalie and that lot. Mr Roberts[1] and Mr Barratt[2] went and sorted them out.
- 9.30 prizes time! Best dancers judged by Miss Boyce[3] – Tom and Kelly. Best dressed students judged by Mrs Headingley[4] (like she'd know) – Adam and Shreya
- 10.00 end – all the lights came on. Becky dancing with Rob!!! Does Gary know??!
- Floor was covered in squashed cups and bits of biscuit
- Everyone went home – said it was really good

1 Head of Year 9
2 Technology teacher
3 PE teacher
4 Maths teacher

1 You have been asked to write an article for your school's student newspaper, reporting on the end-of-term disco.

   a Look at the notes above and on page 43. Which of the facts would you put in your report? Which would you leave out? Remember, the audience for the article is students in your school.

   b Write two or three sentences giving reasons for your decisions. For example, you might decide to leave out some details because you think that they are:

   • not interesting for this audience
   • irrelevant
   • too personal to be published
   • just the writer's opinion
   • another reason.

Develop your awareness of your audience.

 ACTIVITY 2

1 Your article for the student newspaper was a great success. Well done! Your Head of Year was so impressed, she has now asked you to write a report on the disco for the school newsletter which is sent to parents and governors.

   a Which of the details you selected for the student newspaper would you include?

   b Which of the details you selected for the student newspaper would you leave out?

   c Are there any details you left out of the student newspaper article which you would include in the school newsletter report?

   d Write two or three sentences explaining the difference between the audiences for these two pieces of writing – the student newspaper and the school newsletter – and how this affected the details you selected for each one.

Choose how to present your selected points.

 ACTIVITY 3

1 Look at these two extracts. One is from the student newspaper and the school newsletter.

A

When it started, the place was empty, just a few kids hanging around. There were more teachers than kids! But by 8 o'clock the place was heaving and the music was pumping.

B

Although it was a little slow to get going, attendance at the disco was very good. Over one hundred students came to the event, supervised by a large number of staff.

   a Which of the extracts do you think is taken from the student newspaper?

   b Which of the extracts do you think is taken from the school newsletter for parents?

   c Write two or three sentences explaining your answer. Aim to comment on the writer's choice of detail as well as their language choice.

2 Look at this detail taken from the notes in Activity 1.

> couldn't move on the dance floor - bit sweaty and smelly!!

Now look at how three different writers chose to include this detail:

A

> It was way too hot and crowded – blimey it stank.

B

> The dance floor was jammed full and everyone was working up a sweat.

C

> The hall was extremely full and, after a short time, there was a very strong odour of perspiration.

Which of these do you think is appropriate for:

a the student newspaper
b the school newsletter
c neither?

For each one, write a sentence or two explaining your answer.

Use a range of details to plan writing appropriate to your audience.

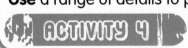
ACTIVITY 4

1 Look at this planning for a piece of writing about your recent French exchange trip.

- My exchange partner was OK but hardly ever spoke.
- Host family's house was nice but in the middle of nowhere.
- Ferry was awful – sick three times!
- French food is really nice.
- Loads of things to do in the nearby town: swimming, cinema, bowling, etc.
- Went and saw a film in French – didn't understand much of it!
- I spoke lots of French – I'm getting better!

Complete the tasks below, selecting and presenting the details in a way which is appropriate to your audience.

a plan and write an email to a friend, telling them about your trip

b plan and write the thank-you letter to your host family which your teacher has asked you to write.

IMPROVING YOUR LEVEL

Level 3	Level 4	Level 5	Level 6
Select points which are generally relevant to the task	Select points which are appropriate to the task and its audience	Present your selected points in a style appropriate to your audience	Select your points and writing style, considering their likely impact on your audience

REMEMBER

- **Gather** all the relevant points for your writing.
- **Select** the points which are appropriate to your audience.
- **Present** your chosen points in a way which is appropriate to your audience.

2.4 Presenting your opinion

What am I learning?

You are learning how to give your opinion in a range of ways.

You need to give your opinion in several types of writing – argument, persuasion, advice, review and analysis. There are lots of different ways of presenting your opinion – and the choices you make can alter the effect you have on your reader.

Look at the way one text presents opinions.

ACTIVITY 1

1 Read the text below. It is taken from a school website.

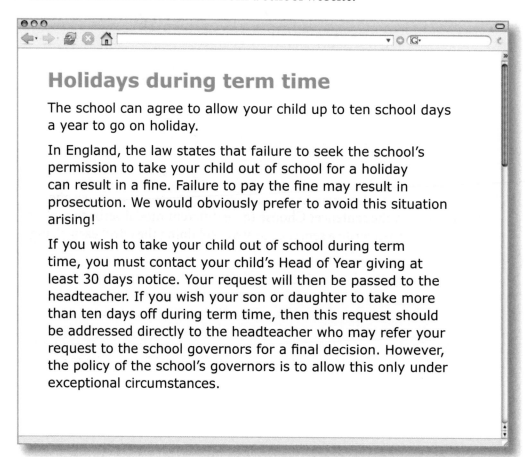

Holidays during term time

The school can agree to allow your child up to ten school days a year to go on holiday.

In England, the law states that failure to seek the school's permission to take your child out of school for a holiday can result in a fine. Failure to pay the fine may result in prosecution. We would obviously prefer to avoid this situation arising!

If you wish to take your child out of school during term time, you must contact your child's Head of Year giving at least 30 days notice. Your request will then be passed to the headteacher. If you wish your son or daughter to take more than ten days off during term time, then this request should be addressed directly to the headteacher who may refer your request to the school governors for a final decision. However, the policy of the school's governors is to allow this only under exceptional circumstances.

2 Modal verbs are often used in writing to advise, when the writer gives their opinion on a range of ways in which problems can be solved or different situations can be tackled. There are eleven modal verbs:

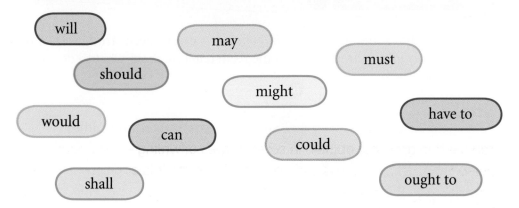

will
may
must
should
might
would
can
have to
could
shall
ought to

How many different modal verbs can you identify in the advice text on page 48?

Develop ways to present your opinion.

ACTIVITY 2

1 You can use modal verbs to change how strongly you express your opinion. Look at this sentence taken from the above text:

> If you wish to take your child out of school during term time, you must contact your child's Head of Year giving at least 30 days notice.

a There is one modal verb in this sentence. What is it?
b What happens to the strength of the writer's opinion if you change the modal verb in the sentence? Choose three different modal verbs to replace the original, then write a sentence or two explaining the effect each change makes.

2 a Which modal verb do you think is the strongest?
   b Which modal verb do you think is the weakest?
   c Put all eleven modal verbs in order from the strongest to the weakest.

3 Write three or four sentences advising all students to complete their homework – and explaining the consequences if they do not. Aim to use as many modal verbs as possible.

> **Choose** the most effective way to present your opinion.
>
>  **ACTIVITY 3**

1 Commands – sometimes called *imperatives* – can be even stronger than modal verbs. They give a direct order to the reader, telling them what to do. For example:

Ⓑ

✂ Cut along the dotted line.

Ⓐ

BUY NOW

Ⓒ

Now wash your hands

Look at the two signs below. Which gets its message across most strongly?

YOU SHOULD KEEP OFF THE GRASS

KEEP OFF THE GRASS

2 Rewrite these sentences using imperatives to replace modal verbs.

a You ought to eat five portions of fruit and vegetables every day.
b You should not sit in front of the television all day.
c You could go swimming or walking or play football with friends.
d You might even enjoy it.

3 Sometimes, writers use the first person (I, me) to express an opinion.

> I think eating meat is wrong because it causes unnecessary cruelty to animals.

Compare it with a similar sentence written in the third person.

> Eating meat is wrong because it causes unnecessary cruelty to animals.

Which of these two sentences presents its opinion more strongly? Why?

4 Sometimes, writers use the first person plural (we, us) to involve and influence the reader. Compare these three different ways of expressing the same opinion.

> People are horrified by cruelty to a dog or cat but they ignore the far greater cruelty involved in producing our food.

> I think that most people are horrified by cruelty to a dog or cat but they ignore the far greater cruelty involved in producing our food.

> We are all horrified by cruelty to a dog or cat but we ignore the far greater cruelty involved in producing our food.

Which sentence would be most effective in influencing the reader's opinion? Why?

5 Choose as many or as few of the jigsaw pieces below to present the opinion as powerfully as possible.

I think that   we must   take action to   stop this now.

Use a range of methods to present your opinion.

1 Look at this list of ways in which we can help to prevent climate change.

- Recycle your rubbish.
- Compost your kitchen waste.
- Walk or cycle rather than use a car.
- Don't waste paper – use both sides.
- Turn off lights when you leave a room.
- Don't leave appliances on standby.
- Turn down your heating, put on a jumper.
- Take a reusable carrier bag to the shops.

2 Use them to complete a short piece of writing to advise entitled:

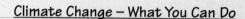

Climate Change – What You Can Do

Aim to present your opinions as effectively as possible, in a range of different ways.

IMPROVING YOUR LEVEL

Level 3	Level 4	Level 5	Level 6
Present your opinion clearly	Use modal verbs to indicate the strength of your opinion	Use modal verbs and imperatives to indicate the strength of your opinion	Choose from a range of methods to present your opinion, eg modal verbs, imperatives, first person

REMEMBER

- **Use** modal verbs to change the strength with which you express your opinion.
- **Avoid** using *I think that...* to express your opinion.
- **Use** 'we' to involve and influence your audience.
- **Use** a range of methods to present your opinion.

2.5 Fact and opinion

What am I learning?

You are learning to use facts and opinions, and to disguise opinions as facts.

A fact is something which can be shown to be true. An opinion is a belief which cannot be proved. Sometimes writers disguise their opinion as fact in order to influence their readers.

Look at how one advertisement uses fact and opinion.

ACTIVITY 1

1   Look at this advertisement for the anti-ageing cream *Nou-You Special FX*.

Nou-You

Special FX Age-Proofing Moisturiser

NEW

A new dawn in younger-looking skin

This concentrated moisturising cream contains scientifically proven natural ingredients including **Alpha Lipoic Acid** and our exclusive **Derma Peptides** to nourish and moisturise your skin. Wrinkles are filled with a complex elastomer. Ageing lines look reduced by up to 37%. Your skin looks fresher, clearer and firmer.

In one month of continued use, see up to 67% reduction in the look of major wrinkles and watch the visible ageing efects of life fade away.

2 Advertisement writers often use statistics as factual evidence to support their claims. Write down two examples of statistics used in this advertisement.

3 Writers sometimes use scientific or technical language to make their opinions more believable and trustworthy. In this advertisement, for example, the writer uses the word *elastomer** Find two other examples of scientific language used in the advertisement.

* a rubber-like, elastic substance

Develop your understanding of fact and opinion.

ACTIVITY 2

1 Sometimes it can be difficult to tell the difference between facts and opinions. For example:

> A new dawn in younger-looking skin

New — This is a fact. The product has only recently been introduced to the *Nou-You* range.

This is an opinion. Some people might disagree.

> see up to a 67% reduction in the look of major wrinkles

It's difficult to tell whether this is a fact or an opinion. The writer has used a statistic which suggests that this is a fact, but it is not clear whether the statistic is based on a survey of people's opinions. How things *look* is often a matter of opinion!

a Look at the advertisement again. Identify three more statements which you think could be a fact *or* an opinion.

b Why did you find it difficult to tell? For each of your examples, decide whether you found it difficult because the writer used:

- statistics
- scientific or technical language
- other people's opinions on, for example, how things *look*.

Choose from a range of ways to disguise your opinion as fact.

ACTIVITY 3

1 Look at this opinion:

> The new Empro V7 football boot helps you score.

Which of these phrases would you add to the opinion to disguise it most effectively as a fact?

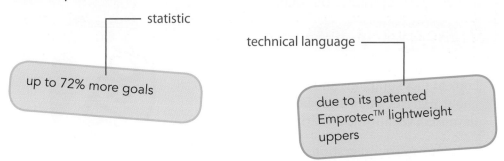

statistic

up to 72% more goals

technical language

due to its patented Emprotec™ lightweight uppers

2   One way in which we recognise a fact is because we know that everyone believes it to be true. For example, very few people would argue that Paris is not the capital of France or that water boils at 26°C. Sometimes writers suggest that everyone knows something to be true in order to make their opinion look more like a fact.

Look at the opinion in the speech bubble below. Which of these sentence starters make this opinion look like a fact?

Obviously,...
Clearly,...
It is widely accepted that...
Everybody knows that...
Only an idiot would disagree that...

Chocolate makes you feel good.

Use a range of methods to present your opinions as facts.

ACTIVITY 3

1 Look at these opinions and statistics about Yogtastic's new strawberry-flavoured, yoghurt health drink.

- Improves your digestion.
- Yoghurt is good for you.
- Makes you feel more energetic by up to 20%.
- Tastes fruity.
- Tastes delicious.
- Contains high levels of the enzyme *Speedioburpatin* to make your digestive tract more efficient.
- Makes you feel ten years younger.

2 Write three or four sentences to advertise the health drink, using a range of different methods to present these opinions as strongly as possible and make them sound like facts.

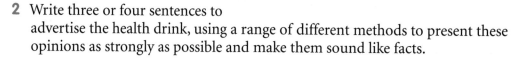
IMPROVING YOUR LEVEL

Level 3	Level 4	Level 5	Level 6
Use facts and opinions in your writing	Use opinions supported with facts to try to influence the reader	Try to disguise your opinions as facts	Choose from a range of methods to disguise your opinions as facts

REMEMBER

- **Use** statistics to support your opinions.
- **Use** scientific or technical language to make you sound like an expert.
- **Use** a range of methods to disguise your opinions as facts.

2.6 Making your mind up

What am I learning?

You are learning how to develop and express your own point of view.

We are surrounded by opinions – from our friends, our parents and from the media. But how do we make our minds up about what **we** think?

Look at a range of opinions.

 ACTIVITY 1

1 A large amount of advertising on television is aimed at children, selling products such as toys, food, drinks, music, films and clothing. Read this article about the different opinions around Europe on advertising aimed at children.

> **credulity:** willingness to believe
>
> **exhort:** encourage

Advertising Aimed at Children

There is a wide range of views around the countries of Europe regarding the rights and wrongs of advertising aimed at children. Most countries agree that some kind of restrictions are needed – but there are significant differences between countries as to the strength and nature of these restrictions.

The European Union currently has 15 member countries. Ten of these nations have strict control on the products which can be advertised and the times at which they can be broadcast. Advertising which targets children under 12 is banned in Sweden. Greece forbids the advertising of children's toys between 7 am and 10 pm and does not allow the advertising of war toys (e.g. toy guns, action figures depicting soldiers) at any time.

The Netherlands, Ireland, France and the UK have clearly stated that, within certain limits, it is acceptable to target advertising at children. The United Kingdom does not permit advertisements that 'might result in harm to children physically, mentally or morally', which may 'take advantage of the natural **credulity** and sense of loyalty of children' or '**exhort** children to purchase or to ask their parents or others to make enquiries or purchases'. France considers that advertisements can prepare children for life, introducing them to the decisions they will need to make as adult **consumers** in a **capitalist society**. Spain has stated that it believes any ban on advertising as an **infringement** of freedom of speech.

One concern which has been repeatedly expressed is the way in which children – particularly young children – can respond to advertising. Evidence strongly suggests that children tend to believe adverts without question. Furthermore, it has been argued that it does not appear to matter whether an advertisement does or does not directly 'exhort' children to pester their parents for a product which appeals to them – if the product appeals, then they will pester. The effect of these demands on a family which does not wish to or cannot afford to buy the product can be stressful.

> **consumers:** people who exchange money for goods or services
>
> **capitalist society:** a society in which it is considered good to make money
>
> **infringement:** a damaging attack or violation

2 a What evidence is there in the text that there should be at least some regulation on advertising aimed at children?

b Why has France not banned advertising aimed at children?

c Why do you think Greece has banned war toys completely?

d Spain has not banned advertising aimed at children because it thinks this would be undemocratic. In what way do you think this would be undemocratic?

e Write down two reasons from the text why advertising aimed at children could be considered unacceptable.

Develop your own opinion.

1 Look at your answers to question in Activity 1. What are the arguments for and against advertising aimed at children? Write them in a table like the one below.

For	Against
Children are much more likely to believe what advertisements tell them.	

2 a What do you think – should advertising aimed at children be banned?
  b Which of the arguments for or against do you agree with?
  c Write two or three sentences explaining your point of view.

Choose a structure to help you present your argument powerfully.

1 When you structure your points in an argument, aim to organise them in a logical sequence. Look at the plan below for an argument entitled *Why We Should Believe in Aliens*. The writer has thought of phrases to link the ideas and check that they follow a logical sequence.

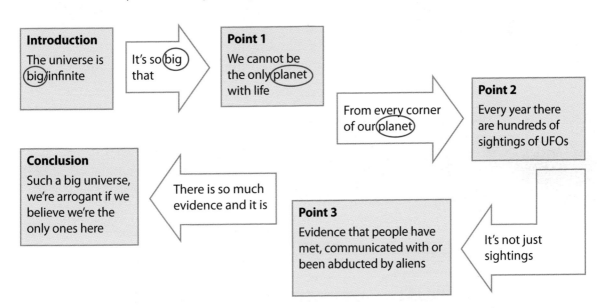

  a Do you think the writer has started with the most powerful argument? Write a sentence or two explaining your answer.
  b Every step in the argument – the introduction, the points, the conclusion and the linking phrases – is connected. The first two connections are shown above. Find the other connections in the rest of the plan.

Use a range of opinions to develop and structure your own opinion.

1 Look at this range of opinions about the benefits of single-sex education – educating boys and girls separately in different schools.

> The behaviour of some boys can stop girls learning.

> Girls take part in lessons much more in single-sex schools – the boys can't drown them out!

> Boys and girls behave much better with an audience of the opposite sex.

> The real world is not single-sex – and school is supposed to prepare us for the real world.

> Exam results show that single-sex schools are not as successful as mixed schools – especially boys' schools.

> Boys and girls distract each other from their education.

a What do you think? Should all our schools be single-sex?
b Identify those arguments with which you agree.
c Use your selected points to structure a short piece of writing to argue that all schools should or should not be single-sex. Aim to:
   • start with your most powerful argument
   • connect the steps in your argument using linking words and phrases.

IMPROVING YOUR LEVEL

Level 3	Level 4	Level 5	Level 6
Aim to express your opinion consistently in your writing	Be sure you consistently maintain your own opinion on the issue you are considering	Develop a range of points which support your opinion	Sequence and connect your points so that the reader can follow them easily

REMEMBER

• **Look** at the arguments for and against.
• **Identify** the arguments with which you agree.
• **Structure** your argument as powerfully as you can.

2.7 The passive voice

What am I learning?

You are learning how to use the passive voice for effect.

It is often said that you should avoid using the passive voice. It can make your meaning less clear and weaken the impact of your writing on your reader. However, there are times when you can use the passive voice to your advantage.

Look at some examples of the passive voice.

We usually use the *active voice* in our writing, for example:

Jason boiled an egg.

... in which

The subject of the verb – the person or thing that is doing whatever the verb describes	is followed by	The verb The thing which is being done	which is followed by	The object The person or thing which is having something done to them

In the *passive voice*, the word order is different and the subject becomes the agent. For example:

An egg was boiled by Jason.

... in which

The object The person or thing which is having something done to them	is followed by	The verb The thing which is being done	which is followed by	The agent of the verb – the person or thing that is doing whatever the verb describes

Which of these sentences are in the *active voice*, and which are in the passive voice?

   a Yusuf cleared the table.
   b The dishwasher was emptied by Ellie.
   c The table was cleared by Yusuf.
   d Ellie emptied the dishwasher.
   e The sink was filled with water.

Develop your use of the passive voice.

1 Look at these sentences taken from an argument entitled *Money Can't Buy Everything*. They are all written in the active voice.

> 1 Everyone needs money.
> 2 You can buy nice food, a nice house and a nice car with money...
> 3 ...but you cannot buy love, friendship and family.
> 4 Poverty might make you unhappy...
> 5 ...but money will not make you happy.

   a Copy out each sentence and label the subject, the verb and the object.
   b Rewrite each sentence in the passive voice.

2 Look again at your answers to question 1. Compare your sentences in the active voice with those in the passive voice. Which do you think makes the writer's meaning clearer: the active or the passive voice?

Choose when and how to use the passive voice to create a range of effects.

You can use the passive voice to change the emphasis of a sentence. For example:

> Money can buy almost anything.

In this sentence, the writer emphasises the importance of money by using the active voice to place it at the start of the sentence.

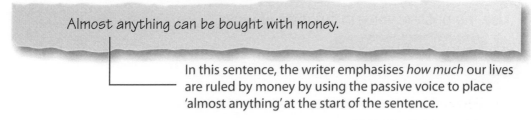

Almost anything can be bought with money.

In this sentence, the writer emphasises *how much* our lives are ruled by money by using the passive voice to place 'almost anything' at the start of the sentence.

1 Look again at your answers to Activity 2. What is emphasised in the original, *active voice* version of each sentence? What is emphasised in your rewritten, *passive voice* version of each sentence?

2 You can use the passive voice to 'hide the agent' – to avoid telling the reader who the subject of the verb is. Look at these examples taken from an argument that *Students should be paid to go to school.*

   • If you don't know who the subject of the verb is; in this case who you think should pay students to go to school:

Active voice

Someone should pay students according to their exam results.

Passive voice

Students should be paid according to their exam results by... er... I'm not sure who, really.

   • If the reader doesn't need to know who the subject of the verb is – or it's so obvious you don't need to tell them:

Active voice

Employers pay adults for the work they do.

Passive voice

Adults are paid for the work they do by their employers

3 Rewrite the sentences below in the passive voice, removing the agent. What effect does it create? The first one has been done for you.

   a Bad behaviour wastes a lot of time at school.

   > A lot of time at school is wasted by bad behaviour.

   b Teachers should teach students the value of money.
   c Businesses and the government would make a lot more money...
   d ...if they spent more money on effective education.

Use the passive voice in a variety of ways.

1   a   What's the greatest invention of all time? Write six or seven sentences arguing your opinion.
    b   Check your writing to see how many times you have used sentences in the active voice and how many in the passive voice.
    c   Select two of your sentences in the active voice and change them so they are in the passive voice.
    d   Write a sentence or two explaining the effect of the changes you have made.

IMPROVING YOUR LEVEL

Level 3	Level 4	Level 5	Level 6
Know how to use the passive voice	Use the passive voice in your writing	Use the passive voice when it helps you express your ideas more clearly	Choose to use the passive voice because of its likely effect on the reader

REMEMBER

- The passive voice uses a different word order from the active voice.
- You can use the passive voice to reorganise a sentence and change its emphasis.
- You can use the passive voice to 'hide the agent'.

AF2 Sample Answers:
Levels 3-6

PURPOSE, AUDIENCE AND FORM

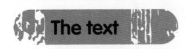

The text   Your school council has received this memo:

> ## MEMO
>
> To: School Council Members
>
> From: the Headteacher
>
> It has been suggested that the school should offer students a wider variety of school trips. I would like you to come up with four or five different suggestions and choose the best one.
>
> You need to suggest trips which would be both enjoyable for students *and* have some educational value.
>
> I cannot promise that we will take you up on your ideas, but we would be very interested to hear them.
>
> Thank you.

The question

> 1 Identify the key words in the question: purpose, audience and form.

Write a letter to the school council, persuading them to choose your idea for a new school trip.

> 2 Identify the Assessment Focus which the question is assessing.

Writing Assessment Focus 2:

Produce texts which are appropriate to task, reader and purpose by:
- identifying the purpose of the task and using its key features
- identifying, and using a register appropriate to, your audience
- using the appropriate form for your writing.

Level 3

- I can usually identify the purpose of the text I need to write.
- I usually try to use some of the key features of that purpose.
- I can write formally and informally but sometimes I forget to use language which is appropriate for my audience.

Hello

I think that Halterford Theme Park would be a good school trip because it would be fun. I have been there with my Mum and it was really good. There are lots of rides you can go on for all ages. My little sister really enjoyed the merry-go-round. I think the trip would be educational because we could ask the theme park to teach us about how all the rides work. I think students would really enjoy this trip. It would be wicked.

> Does not use the appropriate form for a letter: *Dear...*

> Persuasive but does not use essential key feature of persuasion: a series of structured points…

> Generally, an appropriate choice of language with occasional 'slips'.

> … and does not meet the full purpose of the task: a trip for *secondary school* students.

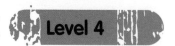

Level 4

- I can always identify the purpose of the text I need to write.
- I always use the key features of that purpose but not always all the way through the piece of writing.
- I usually use a register which suits my audience but not always all the way through a piece of writing.

Dear School Council members

I am writing to suggest a new school trip. I think a visit to Halterford Theme Park would be both educational and enjoyable.

I think this because:

- lots of young people visit the park with their families every year
- there are lots of different kinds of rides
- there is a place at the park where they teach you how everything works which is good for us learning about science and technology.

> Uses an appropriate form for letter writing.

> Good structure: starts with introduction explaining reason for writing, related to task. Could be developed further.

> A more formal register would be more persuasive.

> Lots of persuasive evidence but not organised in paragraphs, supporting clearly made points – a key feature of writing to persuade.

66

Level 5

- I can always identify the purpose of the text I need to write.
- I always use the key features of that purpose throughout the piece of writing.
- I always use a register which suits my audience but occasionally I use language which is too informal.

> Dear School Council Members
> I am writing to recommend a school trip which I think would be fun and educational. I have been on many school trips to several different places such as museums and a castle. Some were quite interesting but usually they were well boring. That is why I am suggesting that we visit the Education Centre at Rydon Park, Halterford United's legendary football ground.
> The Education Centre has lots of facilities which students would find interesting. For example, you can use computers to find out all about the history of football, the club and the ground.

Uses an appropriate form for letter writing.

Uses good structure for persuasive writing: an introduction setting out reasons for writing and initial thoughts on the topic...

Appropriately formal tone...

Oops! Far too informal.

.. followed by first point, supported with evidence.

Level 6

- I always use a wide range of key features for the purpose of the text I need to write.
- Sometimes I adapt them, depending on the audience I am writing for.
- I can develop and express my opinion clearly using a range of techniques.
- I always use a register which suits my audience. Sometimes I vary it for effect.

Appropriate form.

> Dear School Council
> The school trip has always been something to look forward to: a day out of lessons, a change of scene, a break from normal school routine. And then you spend a day trailing round a dusty museum or a ruined castle, looking in glass cases... Boring! You're glad to get back on the coach and go home. And what did you learn? Zilch!
> Clearly, we need to come up with something new, something different.

An effective introduction explores the issue.

Opinion strongly expressed.

Uses informal register for effect.

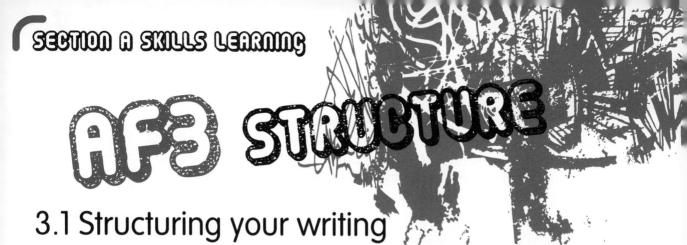

AF3 STRUCTURE

3.1 Structuring your writing

What am I learning?

You are learning to organise the structure your writing.

A good piece of writing has a beginning, a middle and an end – but the job done by each of those parts depends on the purpose of the text. When you write to argue, persuade or advise, to review or analyse, to inform or explain, you need to begin with an introduction, end with your conclusion and make your key points in the middle.

Look at a range of introductions and conclusions.

ACTIVITY 1

Look at these four paragraphs taken from two pieces of students' writing. Which two are introductions and which two are conclusions?

A
> Twenty years ago, nearly 20% of people in the United Kingdom were classed as overweight. That figure has now doubled to nearly 40%. Even more worryingly, 19% of people in the United Kingdom are not just overweight – they're obese. Clearly, we are getting fatter and fatter.

B
> There is more to life than school. There is more to education than school. What about learning to get on with other people, to enjoy ourselves? If we are going to grow up into happy human beings, we need to spend more time learning how, and spend less time in school.

C Attending school between the ages of five and sixteen is compulsory by law. Thirty nine weeks a year, five days a week, six hours a day, we come to school. That's one thousand one hundred and seventy hours we spend in school every year. Is this a good use of our time?

D Being overweight is not just about how we look. It's about how long we live, and how we die. If we don't eat more healthily and take more exercise, we are more likely to develop heart disease, high blood pressure, diabetes, some cancers, Alzheimer's disease, and several other medical problems. If we don't do more in school to educate students about how to eat healthily, offering them healthy food, offering them more opportunities to get active and fit, we may live to regret what we and our children have become.

Develop your understanding of introductions and conclusions.

1 An introduction introduces the subject of a piece of writing. It can:
- give background information on the subject, using facts or statistics
- introduce the key point the writer is making.

Identify sentences in which the writer has used either of these elements in the two introductions above. Write your answers in a table like this:

	Example: Introduction 1	Example: Introduction 2
Gives background information		
Introduces the key point		

2 A conclusion sums up a piece of writing. It can:
- give the writer's opinion and try to influence the reader's opinion
- state what the writer thinks will happen if we do (or don't) follow their suggestions.

Identify sentences in which the writer has used either of these elements in the two conclusions above. Write your answers in a table like this:

	Example: Conclusion 1	Example: Conclusion 2
Gives the writer's opinion		
States what the writer thinks will happen		

Choose the elements to include in your introductions and conclusions.

ACTIVITY 3

1 Look at writing tasks A and B and the notes which a student has made in preparation for them.

You have been asked to contribute to a new magazine for teenagers. Write a review of a favourite book, DVD, TV programme or computer game which you think would appeal to its readers.

TV programme: Friends
- Exciting cliffhangers make you want to watch next episode
- Makes you laugh and cry
- All about their relationships, jobs, adventures
- US situation comedy tells story of six friends living together
- Set in New York
- One of the most popular, long running sitcoms ever.
- Favourite character: Joey; he's funny because he says/does stupid things
- Lots of famous guest stars

B

Your school is thinking about changing the structure of the school year: a four-week Christmas holiday, a ten-week summer holiday, and two twenty-week terms. Write a letter to the school governors giving your views on this.

- At the moment: six terms with holidays varying between one week and six weeks
- Students and teachers look forward to the holidays
- How will twenty-week terms affect everyone?
- Long terms – teachers/students may get tired and bored
- We will learn less for last few weeks of very long term
- Students always get bored in six-week summer holiday
- Better to have shorter terms and more frequent holidays
- Illness and truancy may increase

a For each task, which of the student's points would you:
  - use in the introduction
  - use in the conclusion
  - use in the middle, or *main body*, of your writing
  - not use at all?

b An effective introduction grabs the reader's attention from the first sentence. An effective conclusion finishes with a strong and memorable opinion. In what order would you use the points you identified in question 1a? Write a sentence or two explaining your decisions.

Use a range of elements in writing introductions and conclusions.

ACTIVITY 4

Plan and write an introduction and a conclusion for each of these two writing tasks.

A

> Write a letter to your favourite celebrity, persuading them to judge your school talent competition.

B

> The area where you live has been nominated for The Happiest Place in Britain Awards. Write a letter to the judges, arguing that they should choose your area as the winner.
>
> Use labels and arrows to identify if and where you have:
>
> - given background information on the subject, using facts or statistics
> - introduced your key point
> - given the writer's opinion and tried to influence the reader's opinion
> - stated what you think will happen if we do (or don't) follow your suggestions.

IMPROVING YOUR LEVEL

Level 3	Level 4	Level 5	Level 6
Signal the opening and closing of your writing	Include an introduction and conclusion in your writing	Use the key features of an introduction and a conclusion to give your writing more impact	Plan and select the points you will use in your introduction and conclusion

REMEMBER

- **Use** the key elements of an introduction and conclusion.
- **Plan** your introduction and conclusion before you start writing.
- **Try** to grab your reader's attention from the start, and finish with something which the reader will remember.

3.2 Layout and presentation

What am I learning?

You are learning to adapt layout and presentation to your purpose and audience.

It is not just the words you choose which can affect or influence your reader. When you are creating a media text such as a leaflet, an advertisement or a webpage, you need to select and adapt its layout and presentation according to the effect you want to create.

Look at the presentation and layout of a leaflet.

ACTIVITY 1

1 Before planning changes to the school curriculum, the government wanted to find out what school students thought should be changed. Look at the extract from a leaflet on page 74, aimed at finding out the views of secondary school students. Think about its:

- **content:** what the text is about
- **layout:** the way the words and images are organised
- **presentation:** the choice of colour, font and images.

Do you and your friends have ideas about how you could make your school better?

This leaflet will give you ideas about the things you might like to discuss and also shares ideas that other students have had. So get your friends or class-mates together and start talking about the differences you can make.

Here are some ways you could find out what others think.

- Talk to students from other schools
- Put up a paper graffiti wall
- Have discussions in tutor group time
- Write articles for your school newspaper
- Have a comments box
- Hold a lunchtime debate

What do you think about ...

... how you are taught?

How do you learn best? Do you like to work things out yourself or have them explained by someone?

Look at the comments below and think about what you could do to improve things for yourself and your classmates. Would you agree with these comments?

- The way teachers teach can make a big difference to how you feel about a subject.
- Students rate highly a teacher's confidence in their subject and their skill in using ICT.
- Young people feel strongly about how their teachers deal with bad behaviour. They value fairness and consistency.

... what you learn?

Do you enjoy what you're learning in school? Do you think it's preparing you for life?

Here are some questions to use as a starting point when you're talking with your friends and classmates.

Q. Do you want to have some choice in what you learn?

Q. Can you understand how the things you're learning will be useful to you? Is this important or not?

Q. What would you like to learn?

Q. What do you think about homework? Is it a waste of time? Does it improve your learning? Do you enjoy the challenge of working by yourself?

'I'd like to learn everyday skills for everyday situations like what to do if I'm given the wrong change in a shop and how to complain.'

a Which of these presentational features chosen to appeal to the intended audience or reflect the text's content can you identify in the leaflet?

- colours • fonts • images

b Which of these layout features used to organise the leaflet's content can you identify in the leaflet?

- text boxes • bullet points • numbered lists

c Can you identify any other layout or presentation features which have been chosen to help organise content, appeal to the intended audience or reflect the text's content?

Develop your understanding of the effect of layout and presentation.

1 Choose at least **three** of the layout and presentation features listed below. For each one, write a sentence or two explaining why you think the writer chose to present and organise the text in this way.

- Image of school students talking.
- Image of girl on mobile phone looking at a book.
- The background image of sky/clouds.
- The speech bubble in the bottom right-hand corner.
- Font which looks like handwriting.
- Bullet points for lists.

2 Do you think the layout and presentation of the leaflet are effective? How would you change them to make it even more appealing for its intended audience of secondary school students?

Choose from a range of presentational and layout features.

1 You have been asked to design a similar leaflet, giving the same information and asking the same questions, but aimed at **primary** school children. What changes would you make to the layout and presentation? Write about:

a the illustrations
b the background image
c the fonts
d how text boxes are used to organise the leaflet's content
e the way in which the leaflet is organised and laid out.

You could use images and fonts collected from magazines and newspapers, draw your own, or write a short description of them. Write a sentence or two explaining each of your decisions.

Use a range of presentational and layout features.

ACTIVITY 4

Your local youth club is organising its first-ever summer camp for 11-to 14-year-old members. You have been given the information and images below. Using the most appropriate information and image, design a leaflet to persuade members to sign up for the five-day camp.

Oakvale information

- 35 acres of campsite and outdoor activities.
- Set in rolling fields and woodland, in the beautiful county of Southshire.
- Activities available include: rope courses, rock climbing, abseiling, canoeing, archery, orienteering, raft building, all with qualified instructors.
- Shop on site selling provisions, confectionery and newspapers.

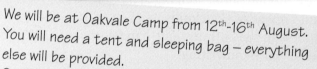

We will be at Oakvale Camp from 12th-16th August. You will need a tent and sleeping bag – everything else will be provided.
Cost including food and all activities: £45.
Deadline for payment: 31st May.

IMPROVING YOUR LEVEL

Level 3	Level 4	Level 5	Level 6
Use some presentational features when appropriate	Use a range of presentational features when appropriate	Select the presentational features in your text so that they are appropriate to your audience	Choose the presentational features in your text, considering their likely impact on your audience

REMEMBER

- **Use** the key features of presentation and layout.
- **Choose** colours, fonts and images which will appeal to your audience and reflect the text.
- **Use** a range of layout features to organise information, for example, text boxes, bullets and numbered lists.

3.3 Connectives

What am I learning?

You are learning to develop your use and range of connectives.

A connective is a word or phrase which you can use to link and develop ideas in your writing. You can use them to connect two clauses in one sentence; or to connect ideas in separate sentences.

Look at a text that uses connectives.

1 Some of the simplest connectives are *and*, *but* and *so*. They are used to link ideas in sentences. Read this extract from one student's writing, in which they have been asked to give advice to teachers on how to make their lessons more interesting.

> How to Make Lessons More Interesting for Students
> Teachers can make you copy off the board and you just sit in lessons and write in silence and you get very bored so you stop concentrating but sometimes we work in pairs and have to talk to each other so that's much more fun and I think teachers should do that kind of thing more often.

  a How many times has this student used the connectives *and*, *but* and *so*?
  b This student uses too many connectives to link all his ideas into one huge sentence. Rewrite the extract, taking out **some** of the connectives and using more full stops. For example:

> Teachers can make you copy off the board ~~and~~. ~~y~~You just sit in lessons and write in silence ~~and~~. ~~y~~You

  c What do you think is a good number of connectives to use in one sentence?

Develop your range of connectives.

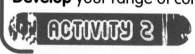

Different connectives do different jobs.

and: **adds** an idea or point in your sentences:

> We should eat healthy food (and) get plenty of exercise.

but: **qualifies** or limits an idea or point in your sentences:

> I like dogs (but) I couldn't eat a whole one.

so: **indicates the effect** or consequence of an idea or point in your sentences:

> I was tired (so) I went to bed.

1 There are many more connectives which do the same jobs. Look at this connective bank:

Connective bank 1		
adding	**qualifying**	**effect**
and	but	so
as well as	however	therefore
moreover	although	consequently
furthermore	yet	thus

2 Rewrite the sentences below, using a range of different connectives. You may need to do more than simply change the connective. For example, you could rewrite:

I love homework <u>so</u> I save it all up for the weekend.
as:

> I love homework. <u>Consequently</u>, I save it all up for the weekend.

   a We should try not to waste paper and we should recycle all the paper we use.
   b You should brush your teeth twice a day and you should floss regularly.
   c I have to be home by 9 o' clock but I can stay out later at the weekend.
   d Everyone knows vegetables are good for you but not everyone likes them.
   e Thousands of people protested so the law had to be changed.
   f My little sister was naughty so she had to go to bed.

Choose from a wider range of connectives.

Connectives can also be used to:

- emphasise

> Social networking websites are extremely popular, <u>especially</u> with teenagers. <u>Similarly,</u> instant messaging services are widely used. Many people see danger in these services, <u>whereas</u> others feel they help develop communication skills and friendships. <u>For example,</u> Aaron, aged 14, said that he had been using a networking website for the last…

- compare

- contrast

- illustrate

Choose a range of connectives from Connectives banks 1 and 2 to link the points at the bottom of this page. You may want or need to change the order of the points and add words or phrases to help connect them.

Connectives bank 2	
Emphasising	**Comparing**
above all in particular especially	in the same way similarly likewise
Contrasting	**Illustrating**
whereas alternatively on the other hand	for example such as for instance

We see advertising everywhere we look.

Leaflets, billboards and websites bombard us with instructions to 'buy now'.

In one hour-long programme on a commercial TV channel we spend 12 minutes watching advertisements.

We cannot escape from advertising on the television.

Many people feel that the advertisements are better than the programmes and look forward to them!

If we did not have advertising to pay for programme-making, the television licence fee would be enormous.

It is important for the UK economy that businesses have an opportunity to sell their products to the widest possible audience.

Use a range of connectives.

Use these questions to help you prepare your own short piece of writing on:

How to Make Lessons More Interesting for Students

What kinds of activities do you **like** doing in lessons? Why?

Do these activities help you learn? Why?

What kinds of activities do you **dislike** doing in lessons? Why?

Do these activities help you learn? Why?

Use your ideas and a range of connectives to write two paragraphs giving your views.

IMPROVING YOUR LEVEL

Level 3	Level 4	Level 5	Level 6
Use connectives such as *and, but, so*	Use a wider range of connectives, eg *however, consequently*	Use a range of connectives to help your reader follow your writing	Select from a range of connectives, considering how they will help your reader follow your writing

REMEMBER

- Do not use too many connectives in any one sentence.
- Connectives do a number of different 'jobs'.
- Aim to use a range of connectives.

3.4 Joined-up writing

What am I learning?

You are learning to use a variety of different methods to link your ideas and give your writing **cohesion**.

> **cohesion:** the links that hold a written or spoken text together

There is a difference between an effective piece of writing and a group of sentences on the same page. An effective piece of writing uses linking words and phrases to guide the reader through the writer's points or ideas, showing how they are connected, and so developing and building them into a whole text.

Look at a whole text.

ACTIVITY 1

> **lamentable:** sad, upsetting

Read this newspaper article in which the writer argues that we should think more about children's behaviour and less about children's rights.

Children's rights?
What about the rights of those who live in fear of young thugs?

Yesterday Sir Al Aynsley-Green, the Children's Commissioner for England, accused the police of treating young people as 'easy prey' to boost their crime statistics… It would have been nice if he had expressed deep concern instead about the way in which rising numbers of ever-younger children are terrorising the public. It would have been pleasing had Sir Al focused his distress upon the truly lamentable state of affairs where people in Britain now think twice before confronting a misbehaving 12-year-old in case he pulls a knife on them.

So many children are now carrying weapons that schools are bristling with metal detectors. The Home Secretary is to announce today, in yet another initiative to deal with rising crime, that parents must allow their children to be searched on school premises at any time. In recent weeks we have seen a sickening stream of cases in which teenagers, often high on drink and drugs, have been attacking people in acts of random savagery and sadism.

Sir Al bangs on about 'children's rights'. But what about the rights of those whose lives are made an absolute misery as a result of the hooliganism, thefts and assaults committed by these children? The idea that the police are oppressing such young people would be hilarious were it not so tragically out of touch.

For the brutal truth is that the police have

in large measure abandoned control of the streets to gangs of out-of-control youths. When they do collar them, they often let them off with a caution; those few who get to court are set free with what is laughably called a community sentence. …

The single most important reason why our children are out of control is the widespread collapse of the parenting role at home and the 'in loco parentis' role once played by teachers, police officers and the courts. Proper parenting involves giving children clear boundaries for their behaviour and showing them that breaching those boundaries has unpleasant consequences for them … Instead of being socialised into adulthood, they remain trapped in a permanent state of **infantilism**. …

We don't need Children's Commissioners. What we do need is parents who actually parent, teachers who teach, policemen who police and courts that enforce the law. We need, in short, a properly functioning society composed of responsible adults with their heads screwed on the right way. Sir Al Aynsley-Green unfortunately shows us that this is precisely what we haven't got.

From the *Daily Mail*, February 2008

breaching: breaking

infantilism: being like a child

Develop your use of linking words and phrases.

ACTIVITY 2

KEY POINT AHEAD

Linking words and phrases can be used to guide or *signpost* the reader through a text. They can:

* indicate the point in time to which the writer is referring
* introduce key points or opinions
* introduce the writer's closing opinion or conclusion.

Which of these three 'jobs' do the words and phrases below taken from the extract above do?

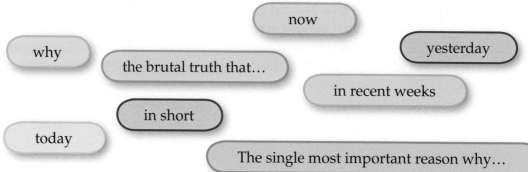

now

why

yesterday

the brutal truth that…

in recent weeks

in short

today

The single most important reason why…

Choose from a wider range of linking words and phrases.

 **ACTIVITY 3**

1 Another way in which you can link ideas in your writing is through repeating patterns of language – using similar words in a similar order. Look again at the first paragraph of the extract on page 81.

   a Write down the two phrases which have a similar language pattern.

   b What effect does this repetition have?

2 The writer also uses repetition at the start of the final paragraph.

   a Write down the two phrases which have a similar language pattern.

   b What effect does this repetition have?

3 In the final paragraph, the writer repeats two phrases which she used in the first paragraph.

   a What are they?

   b How does this help to create *cohesion* in the text?

Use a range of words and phrases to link points and ideas in your writing.

 **ACTIVITY 4**

1 **a** Do you think that...

     • the public are being terrorised by children?

     • so many children carry knives that schools are 'bristling with metal detectors'?

     • parents, teachers and police officers are doing their jobs properly?

   b Write a short newspaper article, arguing your point of view in response to the extract on pages 81 and 82. Aim to use a range of the techniques, and the linking words and phrases which you explored in Activity 2 and Activity 3 in order to:

     • indicate the point in time to which you are referring

     • introduce your key points

     • introduce your conclusion

     • emphasise and build up your points

     • link your conclusion to your introduction.

IMPROVING YOUR LEVEL

Level 3	Level 4	Level 5	Level 6
Use some linking phrases, eg *Then, next*	Use a wider range of linking phrases, eg *Another reason why... I also think that...*	Use a range of linking words and phrases to help your reader follow your writing	Select from a range of linking words and phrases, considering how they will help your reader follow your writing

REMEMBER

- Use a range of linking words and phrases to give your writing cohesion.
- Cohesion helps the reader follow the development of your points and ideas.

AF3 Sample Answers: Levels 3-6

STRUCTURE

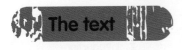

The text — Read this article which has appeared in your school newsletter.

Greener transport

The school governors are looking for ways in which we can make our school more environmentally friendly. A recent survey carried out by the local council has shown that nearly 50% of our students travel to and from school by car, causing enormous amounts of unnecessary pollution. The governors are suggesting that we introduce measures to discourage students from travelling by car, and encourage them to walk, cycle, use public transport or school buses. The governors would like to know what parents and students think on this matter. Please send your views, either by post to the school address or by email to governors@yourschool.southshire.sch.uk.

The question

> 1 Identify the key words in the question: purpose, audience and form.

Write a letter to the school governors arguing for or against this idea. You could write about:
- how it will affect students in your school
- the problems it would cause
- the benefits it would have.

> 2 Identify the Assessment Focus which the question is assessing. Almost any writing task can be assessed on its organisation and structure

Writing Assessment Focus 3:

Organising and presenting whole texts effectively by:
- using an effective opening and ending
- effectively sequencing points and ideas
- linking points and ideas using a variety of connectives.

Level 3

- Sometimes I find it difficult to decide on the best order for my ideas.
- I try to make sure my opening and ending suit what I am writing.
- Sometimes it is difficult for readers to follow the ideas in my writing because I do not always link them.

I think it would be a bad idea to stop students coming to school by car. But it might be a good idea in some ways. Some people cannot get a bus and they live too far away to walk or cycle so they have to come by car and if they didn't come by car they would not be able to come to school. Also, buses are really expensive. Going back to what I said earlier, it might be a good idea because traffic outside school in the morning is really bad.

Introduction introduces the key argument but does not give the writer's opinions very clearly.

Uses too many simple connectives to link too many ideas into one very long sentence.

Linking phrase used as signpost but shows that ideas have not been logically sequenced.

Connective used but the point is not linked or in a logical order.

Level 4

- I usually organise the information, ideas or events in my writing. I usually make sure my opening and ending suit what I am writing.
- I usually structure my writing by putting things in a logical order.
- Sometimes I forget to link my paragraphs or use connectives to help the reader follow my ideas.

Dear School Governors
I read the recent school newsletter and am writing about discouraging students from coming to school by car. I think this is a good idea.
Every morning there are hundreds of cars queuing up outside school and it makes it really difficult for the school buses. Some students are late to school because of this.
School buses come from all around school so most people would be able to catch one.

Introduction clearly indicates the background of the subject and introduces the argument.

Logical sequence of ideas, developing the argument...

...but no connective or linking phrase to signpost development of ideas.

Level 5

- I organise the information, ideas or events in my writing clearly.
- I usually plan the whole piece of writing before I begin, thinking about how my ideas relate or connect to each other.
- I usually link my paragraphs using connectives to help the reader follow my ideas.

> My final point is that some students do not have a bike and may not be able to afford one. Because the roads are so busy, some people don't like their children riding bikes because they think it's dangerous.
>
> If we want to discourage students from travelling to school by car, we will have to make sure that these problems are solved. We will have to increase the number of school buses and ask the bus company to change their timetables so that every student can come to school on time.

Connective used as 'signpost' to guide the reader through the argument.

No connective linking two related points.

An effective conclusion, summing up the writer's argument and suggesting what needs to be done.

Linking phrase refers back to previous paragraphs.

Level 6

- I always organise the information, ideas or events in my writing, thinking about the effect I want to have on the reader.
- I help the reader follow my ideas in a variety of ways: I use connectives, clear opening sentences in paragraphs, and links between paragraphs.

> Everyone should be worried about the environment and how cars add to the problem. However, stopping students coming to school by car would cause problems for lots of people every day.
>
> The greatest problem would be that many students cannot come to school in any other way. For example, I live seven miles from school. There is no school bus from where I live and the only other bus leaves too late.

Clear introduction considering the argument.

Connectives and linking phrases used in and at start of paragraphs clearly 'signpost' development of ideas.

Logical sequence of points making the writer's argument very clear.

AF4 PARAGRAPHS

4.1 What is a paragraph?

What am I learning?

You are learning to organise your writing in paragraphs to support meaning and for effect.

Imagine trying to cut your food into bite-sized pieces without a knife and fork. In the same way, a reader is likely to be put off reading by a page of solid writing. With no breaks at all, the writing looks hugely daunting and uninviting. Using paragraphs makes your writing look organised and more digestible, as well as helping the reader to follow your meaning.

Look at when to start a new paragraph.

ACTIVITY 1

There are four reasons to start a new paragraph:

- a new subject or topic
- a new time
- a new place or setting
- a new speaker.

For which of the four reasons above did these writers start a new paragraph?

A Exactly the same thing happened the next day.

B 'No I haven't!' she cried. 'How could you say such a thing?'

C Melissa arrived at school, still wondering what Sian's message meant.

D The most important thing to consider is, of course, the cost.

Develop your paragraphing skills.

 **ACTIVITY 2**

1 A paragraph can contain one sentence or 20 – although three to five sentences is probably about average. Look at this story which the writer has forgotten to paragraph.

The sun was shining and there wasn't a cloud in the sky. Scott was watching television. 'It's a lovely day, Scott,' said his mum. 'We should go somewhere, to the park, maybe. Would you like that?' 'No.' 'I'm sure your sister will want to go,' said his mum. Scott's little sister, Aimee, was in the garden collecting worms. She had tried eating one but decided it didn't taste as nice as it looked. Mum called her in and they headed off to the park together. It was lunchtime before Scott realised they should have been back hours ago.

Where should the writer have started a new paragraph? Write down the first word of each new paragraph.

2 Look at this writer's plan for the opening of a short story.

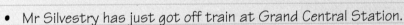

- Mr Silvestry has just got off train at Grand Central Station.
- Walks nervously along platform, looking over shoulder.
- Mr S. reads newspaper in station cafe, looking for apartment to rent
- In Chicago, Gangster Boss and cronies are playing cards. Mugsy runs in: says Silvestry has disappeared. Boss looks angry.
- Mr S. arrives at his new apartment. It's damp and dirty. He tells landlady Mrs Kowalski he'll take the room. She says visitors not allowed after 9pm. He says he hopes he won't be having any visitors! She leaves. He locks the door, opens his suitcase and counts the piles of dollar bills it contains.

When should the writer start a new paragraph? Copy out the writer's plan, putting a double slash (//) to show where you think each new paragraph should start.

Choose your paragraph structure for effect.

You can create a range of different effects by choosing how you structure your paragraphs. Look at these two pieces of writing:

A **Marie Antoinette**

Maria Antonia Josepha Johanna von Habsburg-Lothringen (2 November 1755 – 16 October 1793), known to history as Marie Antoinette, was born an Archduchess of Austria and later became Queen of France and Navarre. At fourteen, she was married to Louis-Auguste, Dauphin of France, the future Louis XVI. She was the mother of Louis XVII, who died in the Temple Tower at the age of ten during the French Revolution. Marie Antoinette is perhaps best remembered for her death: she was executed by guillotine at the height of the French Revolution in 1793 for the crime of treason.

B **The House on The Hill**

The front door creaked and slammed behind him, blowing a cloud of dust through his hair and leaving him with only the light from one broken, dirty window. He climbed the stairs, slowly, treading more and more nervously with each creak and groan from their rotting wood, until he arrived at the top. A corridor stretched ahead, lined with closed doors and darkness. At the end of the corridor, in the distance, one door was open. Through the darkness within, a candle burned.

He was not alone.

In the two extracts above, there are three paragraphs. Two are long, one is very short.

a Which one is written to make the reader want to read on? How?
b Which one is structured to build tension? How?
c Which one is structured to give lots of detailed information? How?
d Which one is written to create dramatic emphasis? How?

Use your paragraphing to create a range of effects.

Look again at the story plan in Activity 2. Write a short extract from the story. Aim to:

- write approximately 200 words
- paragraph correctly, remembering the four reasons to start a new paragraph
- use longer paragraphs to build tension, or give detailed information
- use at least one short, punchy paragraph to create a dramatic moment
- finish each paragraph with a sentence which makes the reader want to read on.

IMPROVING YOUR LEVEL

Level 3	Level 4	Level 5	Level 6
Use paragraphs occasionally	Usually write in paragraphs, starting a new paragraph for a new subject, setting, time or speaker	Consistently write in paragraphs, sometimes thinking about their effect on the reader	Choose the length and structure of paragraphs, considering their likely effect on the reader

REMEMBER

- There are four reasons for starting a new paragraph.
- A paragraph can be as short as a single word.
- You can use longer or shorter paragraphs to give information, to make the reader want to read on, and to create tension and drama.

4.2 Structuring paragraphs

What am I learning?

You are learning to organise your points and ideas in effective paragraphs.

When you write a story, you need to structure your paragraphs according to the effect you want to create. However, when you are writing to argue or advise, to inform or explain, to analyse or review, it is important to structure your paragraphs so that your writing achieves its purpose and can be clearly understood.

Look at two different paragraph structures.

1   Look at the two pieces of writing below. Both are about Internet plagiarism: writers copying information directly from the Internet and pretending it is their own work.

Ⓐ

Writing to argue

> **Is the Internet the Greatest Invention of All Time?**
> There is one major problem when students use the Internet as a source of reliable information. A recent survey of 50 pages in a well known Internet encyclopaedia found an alarming 162 factual mistakes. That's more than three on every page. Clearly if students are relying on cutting and pasting from the Internet instead of doing their own thinking, there are two problems. Firstly, they are not thinking for themselves. Secondly, they are cutting and pasting information which is incorrect.

Point:
states the key point which the writer is making.

Evidence:
supports the point using facts or statistics.

Explain:
explains how the evidence supports the writer's key point.

B

Writing to inform

Pupils plagiarise so much that we receive essays with adverts accidentally copied from Internet, say teachers

Plagiarism is now so common among sixth formers that teachers are receiving identical essays from pupils – some still including adverts accidentally copied from the Internet. More than half of teachers believe that plagiarism is a major problem among A-level pupils, a teaching union warned yesterday. They suspect that students copy much of their work from the Internet and often do not understand what counts as legitimate research.

Topic sentence: states the key point or subject of the paragraph.

Expand: further sentences add more detailed information on the key point or subject of the topic sentence.

2 Which paragraph structure would you use – point-evidence-explain (PEE) or topic-sentence-expand (TSE) – in these kinds of writing?

a Writing to argue
b Writing to persuade
c Writing to advise
d Writing to review
e Writing to analyse
f Writing to inform
g Writing to explain

Develop your paragraph organisation skills.

ACTIVITY 2

1 Look at the sentences below. They are taken from two different paragraphs, one from Text A and one from Text B. One paragraph is organised using point-evidence-explain, the other using topic-sentence-expand. Which sentences have been taken from which text? In what order should they be organised?

a Every day the Internet grows bigger and bigger.

b Gill Bullen, a teacher from Itchen College in Southampton, said: 'Two GCSE English retake students were very late in handing in an essay on *Romeo and Juliet*. When finally given in, their pieces turned out to be identical.'

c It found that 58 per cent believe Internet plagiarism is an issue, fearing that more than a quarter of work handed in includes material copied from Internet sites.

d One recent estimate suggests that there are approximately 170 million websites and a total of 17 billion web pages currently available on the World Wide Web. Research suggests that around 10 million new pages are being added every day.

e The Internet is growing much faster than any of us can read. Surely we do not need this quantity of incorrect information and worthless opinions.

f The Association of Teachers and Lecturers (ATL) questioned around 300 teachers in school sixth forms, sixth-form colleges and further education colleges.

Choose the best evidence to support your point.

 **ACTIVITY 3**

1 a In your writing you should use a range of evidence. You can use:
- facts and statistics
- your personal experience
- anecdotes (stories which demonstrate the point you are making).

Look at this point taken from a later paragraph in Text A on page 92.

> It's very easy to waste hours, even days, on the Internet.

b Which one or more of these pieces of evidence do you think best proves this point?

A
> A recent survey shows the average Internet user spends eleven hours a week online.

B
> I personally can spend three hours on Bebo, chatting to the people I've just spent all day chatting to at school.

C
> I know many teenagers who spend every evening on the Internet, chatting, looking at each other's Bebo pages, copying and pasting their homework, or shopping.

Use an appropriate paragraph structure to organise your writing.

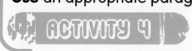

1 Use the evidence and information below about the Internet to write two paragraphs.

   a In one paragraph, inform the reader about the Internet. Use topic-sentence-expand to structure your writing.

   b In the other paragraph, argue that the Internet is a great invention. Use point-evidence-explain to structure your writing.

The Internet
- The World Wide Web was invented by Tim Berners-Lee in 1990.
- It took just five years from its invention for the Internet to reach a total of 50 million users around the world. It took 13 years for television and 38 years for radio to reach this figure.
- Approximately 85 per cent of people living in the UK will look at the Internet in the next year.
- In 2007, Internet shoppers in the UK spent more than 10 billion pounds online.

IMPROVING YOUR LEVEL

Level 3	Level 4	Level 5	Level 6
Don't really consider paragraph structure	Sometimes choose the most appropriate paragraph structure to use and understand the difference between point-evidence-explanation and topic-sentence-expand	Always choose the most appropriate paragraph structure for my writing, making sure to develop my points in some detail	Select evidence from a range of sources, including facts, personal experience and anecdotes

REMEMBER

- Structuring your paragraphs will make your writing clearer and help it achieve its purpose.
- You can structure paragraphs using point-evidence-explain (PEE) or topic-sentence-expand (TSE).
- Develop the structure of your paragraphs by adding additional evidence and explanation.

4.3 Holding it all together

What am I learning?

You are learning to use pronouns and synonyms to give your paragraphs cohesion.

Sometimes writers use repetition for effect. It can be used to emphasise a point or idea, making it more persuasive. More often, though, writers try to avoid repeating the same words in any one paragraph; it can lose their reader's interest and attention. If you give your writing **cohesion** – making your meaning clear and showing how your ideas are linked – you can avoid repeating yourself by using **pronouns** and **synonyms**.

cohesion: the ways sentences are linked together – by meaning, words or grammar

pronoun: a word which can be used to replace a noun or noun phrase

synonyms: different words with identical or similar meanings

Look at two paragraphs of writing.

ACTIVITY 1

1 Read Text A. It is taken from a Year 6 student's writing.

Ⓐ

> The boy took his dog to the park. The boy walked his dog around the park because the boy knew that the dog loved walking around the park. All of a sudden he started running. He ran after him but he could not catch him up and soon he could not see him. He was lost. He had to go home without him. When he got home he found him and started wagging his tail.

How effective do you find this piece of writing? Is it interesting? Is its meaning clear? Write two or three sentences explaining your answer.

2 Read Text B on the following page. It is taken from a newspaper article about famous actors, writers and politicians and their teachers' memories of them. In this extract, J.K. Rowling's science teacher remembers her time at Wyedean Comprehensive in Chepstow.

B

Joanne has said that no characters in Harry Potter are based more than 10 per cent on any one person. I suppose the fact that I used to have long, black hair is just a coincidence. To be honest, I think Snape, especially in the later books, is very like me.

Joanne would have been about 12 when I taught her. Her days at Wyedean were pretty miserable. The school was like a prison, and then her mum came down with MS. Anne Rowling worked as my technician, and Joanne would come and wait at the science block for her mum so they could walk home together. It was obvious the child was very concerned about her mother – preoccupied. She was a very quiet child. I don't remember her ever answering a question – she would go to great lengths to avoid responding. I think she was tucking it all away in her head to use later in her stories.

How effective do you find this piece of writing? Is it interesting? Is its meaning clear? Write two or three sentences explaining your answer.

Develop your use of pronouns.

ACTIVITY 2

1 This sentence can be written in two different ways:

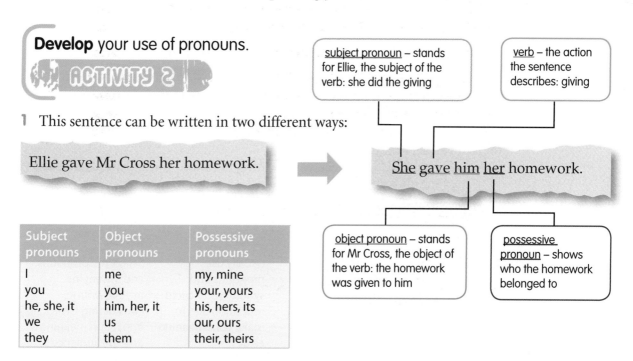

Ellie gave Mr Cross her homework.

She gave him her homework.

subject pronoun – stands for Ellie, the subject of the verb: she did the giving

verb – the action the sentence describes: giving

object pronoun – stands for Mr Cross, the object of the verb: the homework was given to him

possessive pronoun – shows who the homework belonged to

Subject pronouns	Object pronouns	Possessive pronouns
I	me	my, mine
you	you	your, yours
he, she, it	him, her, it	his, hers, its
we	us	our, ours
they	them	their, theirs

a Identify **three** subject or object pronouns in Text B. Which nouns are they replacing or referring to?

b Identify **three** nouns in Text B. Why has the writer **not** replaced them with pronouns?

2 Rewrite the first **two** sentences of Text A on page 96, replacing some of the nouns with pronouns. Try to make the meaning clear, but avoid repeating the nouns and noun phrases.

Choose synonyms and pronouns to give your writing cohesion.

1 The writer of Text B on page 97 uses synonyms to avoid repeating himself. For example, instead of repeating 'Anne Rowling' he uses the noun phrase 'her mum'. Find one other example where the writer uses a synonym.

2 Write down as many synonyms as you can think of in one minute for each of these words:

   a dog   b boy.

3 Rewrite the last five sentences of Text A (from 'All of a sudden...') on page 96, using a range of pronouns and synonyms to give your writing cohesion. Remember: you need to make your meaning clear and avoid repetition of nouns and noun phrases.

Use a range of techniques to give your writing cohesion.

What will your teachers say about **you** when you're rich and famous?

- Imagine you are one of your teachers in 20 years' time, remembering you.
- Write two or three paragraphs, describing your time in their lessons from your teacher's point of view.
- Use a variety of synonyms and pronouns to avoid repeating nouns and noun phrases.
- When you have finished, check your writing to ensure your meaning is clear.

IMPROVING YOUR LEVEL

Level 3	Level 4	Level 5	Level 6
Often repeat words to help your writing make sense	Sometimes use pronouns to avoid repetition and to make my meaning clear	Usually use pronouns and synonyms to avoid repetition and to make your meaning clear	Select the pronouns and synonyms in your writing, considering their impact on meaning and the audience's response

REMEMBER

- **Pronouns** can be used to replace nouns and noun phrases.
- **Synonyms** can be used to avoid repeating nouns and noun phrases.
- Using pronouns and synonyms in your writing gives it cohesion.

AF4 Sample Answers:
Levels 3–6

PARAGRAPHS

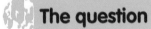

The question

> 1 Identify the key words in the question: purpose, audience and form.

What's it *really* like to be famous? Write an article for a teenage magazine, analysing the advantages and disadvantages of fame.

You could write about:

- the advantages that fame brings
- the problems that fame can cause
- your conclusion: is fame a good thing or a bad thing?

> 2 Identify the Assessment Focus which the question is assessing. Almost any writing task can be assessed on its paragraphing.

Writing Assessment Focus 4:

Constructing paragraphs and using cohesion within and between paragraphs by:

- writing in paragraphs
- effectively sequencing my sentences in paragraphs
- linking sentences and paragraphs using a range of techniques.

Level 3

- Sometimes I organise my sentences into paragraphs.
- Sometimes I link the ideas in my sentences, but I don't use connectives very often.
- Sometimes it is difficult for readers to follow the ideas in my writing because I do not always link them.

It would be good to be famous because you would have lots of money and you can do whatever you want. You can buy a big house and a swimming pool and a nice car. You could go on expensive holidays. You wouldn't have to work very hard to live a good life. You would have your picture in the newspapers and magazines and everyone would want to talk to you and you would be popular.

> A series of unrelated points, not sequenced into structured paragraphs.

> Lots of good ideas but not organised into paragraphs

Level 4

- I usually decide on the order in which I will put the sentences in my paragraphs.
- I use some connectives to link the sentences in my paragraphs – but I often use the same connectives, for example, also, then, so.
- I sometimes link my paragraphs and use connectives to help the reader follow my ideas.

Famous people can earn a lot of money. A Premier League footballer can earn over £100,000 a week. Also, singers earn millions of pounds a year.

One bad thing about being famous is that you are followed everywhere by photographers and you don't have a minute's peace. David Beckham's photo is in the papers every day so he must get his picture taken everywhere he goes.

> Organised in paragraphs, using point and evidence. Adding an explanation would help support and develop each point.

> Sentences are organised in a logical sequence, but linked with a limited use of connectives, for example, also, so.

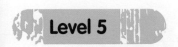

Level 5

- I decide the best way to put my information or ideas into paragraphs.
- I use different ways to link my sentences together in a paragraph. Sometimes I use connectives, sometimes pronouns, and sometimes I refer back to previous ideas.
- I try to write each paragraph so that it fits into the finished piece of writing.

> The best thing about being famous would be meeting lots of other famous people. You would get to meet all the top footballers and singers. Sometimes celebrities even marry each other. For example, Brad Pitt met Angelina Jolie while they were making 'Mr and Mrs Smith'. Later, they got married. Talking to a famous person would be interesting and exciting. Marrying him would be even more interesting and exciting – especially if he was Brad Pitt!

Effectively uses:
• point
• evidence
• explain
to organise sentences in the paragraph.

A range of connectives used.

Uses pronouns to refer back to previous ideas.

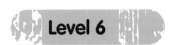

Level 6

- I always organise and write paragraphs so that they help my writing achieve what I want to say and how I want to say it.
- I carefully choose connectives (and other links between sentences) both to connect my ideas and for the effect on the reader I want to achieve.

> Famous people can be put under a lot of pressure. Living in the public eye, with every move watched and photographed, can make celebrities turn to drink or drugs. Elvis Presley, for example, lived on deep-fried peanut butter sandwiches and prescription pills. As a result, he died at the age of 42 weighing nearly twenty stone. Perhaps if he had not been famous, Elvis would be alive and happy today.
>   Is fame worth it?

Effectively uses point-evidence-explain to organise sentences in the paragraph BUT also 'breaks' the structure for effect, using a short paragraph to emphasise a key point.

Uses synonyms and pronouns to give cohesion and avoid repetition.

101

AF5 SENTENCES

5.1 Sentence variety

> ### What am I learning?
>
> You are learning that successful writing is not just about the ideas you use and the language you choose. Varying the structure and length of your sentences can make a significant contribution to the effectiveness of your writing.

Look at the ways in which a writer can vary sentence length for effect.

ACTIVITY I

1 Reading the folowing extract. Eva Delectorskaya is in Edinburgh, training to be a spy. In this extract, she is being followed and must 'lose' the other trainee spies who are following her.

Eva Delectorskaya walked down the sloping street from St Andrews Square and turned right on to Princes Street. She was walking quickly, purposefully, not glancing back, but her head was full of the knowledge that at least six people were following her: two ahead, she thought, doubling back, and four behind, and perhaps a seventh, a stray, picking up instructions from the others, just to confuse her.

She paused at certain shop windows, looking at the reflections, relying on her eye to spot something familiar, something already seen, searching for people covering their faces with hats and newspapers and guidebooks – but she could see nothing suspicious. Off again. She crossed the broad street to the Gardens side, darting between a tram and a **brewer's dray**, running between motor cars to the Scott Monument. She walked behind it, turned on her heel and, picking up speed now, strode briskly back in the opposite direction towards Carlton Hill. **On a whim** she suddenly ducked into the North British Hotel, the doorman having no time to tip his cap to her. At reception she asked to be shown a room and was taken up to the fourth floor. She did not linger as she enquired about rates and where the bathroom was. Outside, she knew, all would be temporary **consternation** but one of them at least would have seen her go into the hotel. Word would be passed. Within five minutes they would be watching every exit.

> **brewer's dray:** a cart delivering barrels of beer
> **on a whim:** on the spur of the moment
> **consternation:** confusion

a Make a list of the streets and landmarks Eva visits on her journey.
b Which is the longest sentence the writer uses in the extract? What does it describe?
c Which is the shortest sentence the writer uses in the extract? What does it describe?

Develop your sentence variety.

1 Verbs change their endings depending on the way they are used in a sentence. Look at this table:

Verb	Past participle	Present participle
walk	walked	walking
run	ran	running
jump	jumped	
fly		

Copy and complete the table, adding the past and present participles of the verbs in the first column.

You can use *present participles* to add detail to a sentence. For example:

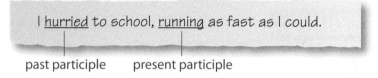

I <u>hurried</u> to school, <u>running</u> as fast as I could.

past participle   present participle

2 Write the next three sentences of the story:

- You reach the school gates.
- You see the empty playground.
- You go to your classroom.

In each of your sentences, use at least **one** past participle and **one** present participle.

Choose from a range of sentences and sentence structures.

1 Look again at these two sentences from the extract.

She paused at certain shop windows, looking at the reflections, relying on her eye to spot something familiar, something already seen, searching for people covering their faces with hats and newspapers and guidebooks – but she could see nothing suspicious. Off again.

a How long do you think Eva spent looking in shop windows? How does the structure of the first sentence show this?

b The writer uses present participles to build up the details in the sentence. What effect do they create?

c The second sentence is very short. What effect does this create?

2 Look at the long sentence below. It uses present participles to add detail and create a feeling.

> I put my foot on the accelerator, pushing the car to its limit, tyres screaming and skidding, the engine roaring at the red light ahead, racing towards me.

a Write a long sentence which could follow the sentence above. Try to use a lot of present participles.

b Write a short sentence which could follow the sentence above.

c What are the different effects of (a) your long sentence and (b) your short sentence?

d Which of your sentences do you think is most effective? Why?

Use a range of sentence structures for effect.

ACTIVITY 4

Write two sentences describing a parachute jump. Aim to use **one long sentence** followed by **one short sentence**.

• What will your final, short sentence describe?

• In the long sentence, try to use a lot of present participles. You could describe: the aeroplane you jumped from, the clouds, the wind, the birds, the ground below you...

floating   blowing   flying

plummeting   racing   roaring

whistling   dropping

IMPROVING YOUR LEVEL

Level 3	Level 4	Level 5	Level 6
Most sentences are about the same length	Use some long sentences and some short sentences	Use different ways, including past participles, to add detail to longer sentences	Use a variety of long and short sentences to create different effects

REMEMBER

- Long sentences, using present participles, can add detail and create a feeling of pace.
- Short sentences can be punchy and dramatic.
- You can vary the length and structure of your sentences to create a range of effects.

5.2 Building sentences

What am I learning?

You are learning to use a range of sentence types for variety and effect.

There are three basic types of sentence. They can be used and combined to create different effects in your writing.

> The three sentence types are:
> • simple
> • compound
> • complex.

Look at three different sentence types.

ACTIVITY 1

Simple sentences contain only one verb, action or event. For example:

> I <u>rode</u> my bike.
>
>   verb

Even if you add lots of descriptive, complex language...

verb

> I dutifully <u>rode</u> my glistening new mountain bike in an appropriately cautious fashion.

...it's still a simple sentence because it contains only one verb.

1   a   Think back to this morning. What were the first four things you did after waking up? Write them in four simple sentences. Remember: each simple sentence should use just **one verb.**

     b   Circle the capital letter, the full stop and the one verb in each sentence.

Compound sentences contain **two** or more verbs. You can make a compound sentence by joining two simple sentences together using the connectives 'and', 'but' or 'so'. For example, the two simple sentences:

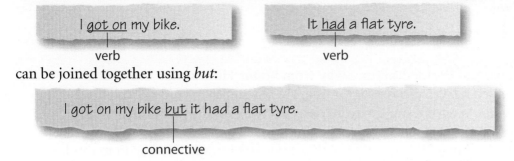

I <u>got on</u> my bike.
verb

It <u>had</u> a flat tyre.
verb

can be joined together using *but*:

I got on my bike <u>but</u> it had a flat tyre.
connective

2 a Join the first two simple sentences you wrote in question 1a to make a compound sentence. Remember to add a connective, and check your full stops and capital letters.
   b Do the same with your third and fourth sentences from question 1a.
   c Circle the capital letter, the full stop, the connective and the two verbs in each sentence.

Complex sentences contain two or more verbs. Like compound sentences, they are made up of two sections or *clauses*: the *main clause* and the *subordinate clause*. They are held together with connectives such as 'if', 'when', 'although' and 'because'. For example:

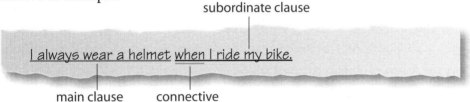

subordinate clause

<u>I always wear a helmet</u> <u>when I ride my bike.</u>
main clause   connective

Notice that:

• The subordinate clause does not make sense by itself: it relies on the main clause to help it make sense.
• You can usually swap the two clauses in a complex sentence around without changing the meaning, for example:

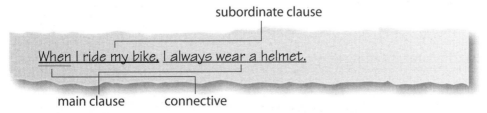

subordinate clause

<u>When I ride my bike,</u> <u>I always wear a helmet.</u>
main clause   connective

3 a Choose two of the simple sentences you wrote in question 1a. Use one of the connectives above to develop both your simple sentences into complex sentences.
   b Circle the capital letter, the full stop, the connective and the two verbs in each sentence.

Develop your use of different sentence types.

ACTIVITY 3

1 Read this story:

> Jake had decided to run away from home. He was not allowed to watch his favourite programme. He felt angry. He did not tell his Mum. He went out the front door. He walked down the street. He did not know where he was going. He felt lost. He felt cold. He had not eaten anything since breakfast. He felt hungry. He began to think about his dinner. He wondered if there would be chips. He looked up at the sky. It was getting dark. He decided to go home. It was not far. He soon found his house. He rang the doorbell. His Mum opened the door. She gave him a big hug.

a The story is written using only simple sentences. Re-write the story, joining some of the simple sentences to make compound sentences, joining some to make complex sentences, and leaving some as simple sentences. Remember to check your capital letters, full stops and connectives.

b Re-write the story again, using a different combination of simple, compound and complex sentences. Which version of the story do you think is most effective?

Choose from a range of sentences.

ACTIVITY 3

Subordinate clauses can go in a range of different places in some complex sentences. The meaning is not changed, but the effect may be. For example:

> He gasped for breath, his legs aching, as he reached the safety of his house.

has the same meaning as:

> As he reached the safety of his house, he gasped for breath, his legs aching.

Sentence A focuses the reader's attention first on the hero's suffering to build tension, and holds back the happy ending, saving it for the end of the sentence. Sentence B, however, focuses the reader's attention immediately on the happy ending, adding the details afterwards.

1 a Which do you think is the more effective sentence?
   b Look at these main and subordinate clauses:

• he fell to the ground
• clutching his chest
• coughing and spluttering
• he tried to speak
• his lips mouthing just one word
• before he lost consciousness

Use the clauses to write one or two complex sentences. Aim to create tension and drama in your writing by carefully choosing the order in which you structure your sentences.

Use a range of sentence structures in a piece of descriptive writing.

1 Imagine a situation in which you are being chased by – or are chasing – someone or something. Write a short description of the chase in eight to ten sentences. Aim to:

• use a range of simple, compound and complex sentences
• choose the sequence and structure of your sentences carefully to give your writing drama and tension.

2 a Identify and highlight **one simple**, **one compound** and **one complex** sentence you have used in your writing.
   b Looking closely at one of your complex sentences, write a sentence or two explaining how you chose to structure it and the effect you wanted to create.

IMPROVING YOUR LEVEL

Level 3	Level 4	Level 5	Level 6
Use simple and compound sentences mainly	Sometimes use complex sentences featuring a limited range of connectives	Use a range of sentence types. Complex sentences feature a range of connectives	Place the subordinate clause in complex sentences, considering its effect on the reader

REMEMBER

• There are three different basic sentence types.
• Use a range of sentence types to give your writing variety.
• Structure and sequence your sentences, thinking about the effect you will create.

5.3 Rhetorical devices

What am I learning?

You are learning how to use a range of rhetorical devices at sentence level.

Rhetorical devices are language techniques or tricks used for effect, often found in persuasive speeches. Some rhetorical devices focus on the language you choose. On these pages, you will be exploring ways of use rhetorical devices to write sentences for effect.

Look at some examples of rhetorical devices.

ACTIVITY 1

A **rhetorical question** answers itself or leads the reader to the writer's desired answer. For example:

> 'And doesn't each of us want to say of ourselves that I helped someone in need? That I come to the aid of a neighbour in distress?'

Gordon Brown, Labour Party Conference, 2008

1   What answer is Gordon Brown expecting to his rhetorical questions?

2   How does Brutus want his audience to respond in the example below?

> 'Who is here so vile that will not love his country?'

From Julius Caesar *by William Shakespeare*

Repetition is a word or phrase repeated to give emphasis. For example:

> 'A horse! A horse! My kingdom for a horse!'

Shakespeare's Richard III *desperate for a horse so that he can rejoin the fight he is losing at the Battle of Bosworth*

3 Identify any *repetition* in this example:

> 'We shall fight in France, we shall fight on the seas and oceans, we shall fight with growing confidence and growing strength in the air... we shall fight on the beaches, we shall fight on the landing grounds, we shall fight in the fields and in the streets, we shall fight in the hills. We shall never surrender.'

Winston Churchill emphasises Britain's commitment to the war, 1940

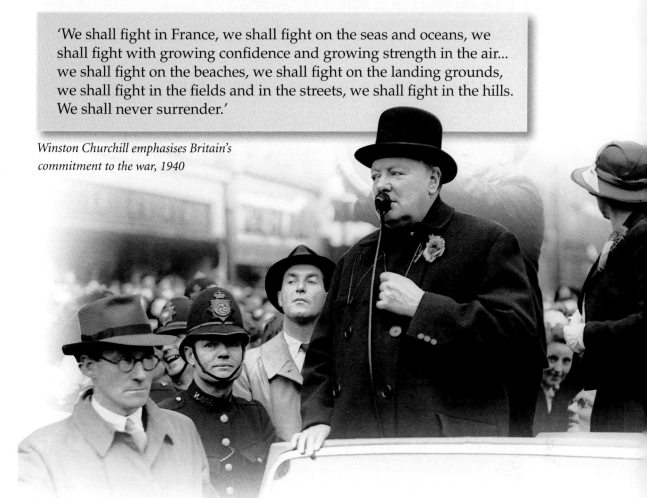

4 What idea is Churchill using this repetition to emphasise?

Pattern of three means three nouns, adjectives or phrases, linked by their structure or language choice. It is used for emphasis. For example:

> **1**   **2**   **3**
> '...government of the people, by the people, for the people'

Abraham Lincoln at the Gettysburg address, 1863, affirming the USA's commitment to democracy

5 Identify the pattern of three in this example:

> 'Never in the field of human conflict has so much been owed by so many to so few'

Winston Churchill thanking the RAF for their contribution to the Battle of Britain, 1940

6 What is Churchill using this pattern of three to emphasise?

Develop your use of rhetorical devices.

1 Read this extract from a student's story entitled *The Box*.

> In the darkest corner of the attic, behind a pile of old newspapers, beneath a thick layer of dust, he noticed a large wooden box. Blowing away the dust, he saw that it was beautifully carved with faces – anxious, worried, frightened faces, shouting faces, screaming faces, howling faces, a living, terrifying crowd of faces. And the box was sealed: barred, bolted and padlocked.

    a Continue the story of *The Box* by adding one or more rhetorical questions.
    b How do your rhetorical questions help draw the reader in to the story?
    c The writer of *The Box* has used several pattern of three structures in her description. Write two of them down. What is the effect of each one?
    d Identify where the writer of *The Box* has used repetition for effect. What effect is she trying to create?
    e Rhetorical devices are like salt on your food: careful use can give your writing flavour, but too much makes it hard to swallow. Has this writer used too many rhetorical devices?

2 Read this extract from a student's persuasive writing on the topic of vegetarianism.

> What if your chicken did not come already cooked in your Chicken Korma and Rice ready meal? What if your chicken did not come killed, cleaned and packaged in a polystyrene tray? What if you had to kill for your dinner? Could you slaughter a live chicken with your bare hands? Killing animals for meat is inhumane, unnecessary, and inexcusable.

    a How many rhetorical questions has the writer used? What effect are they intended to have?
    b The writer has used two pattern of three structures. Write them down. What is their effect?
    c The writer has used repetition for effect. Which words or phrases are repeated? What effect does this have?

Choose from a range of rhetorical devices.

These sentences are from students' persuasive writing on *Giving up smoking*:

- Would you make a bonfire out of newspapers and dead plants and inhale the smoke for fun?
- Why do something which will inevitably kill you?
- Smoking makes your fingers yellow, your clothes smell, and your breath stink.
- Smoking damages your lungs, your heart and your arteries.
- You're burning your body and burning your money.
- Smoking does not make you look cool and it does not make you look clever.

Choose some of these – and add some sentences of your own – to write a persuasive paragraph.

Use a range of rhetorical devices in your writing.

1 a Write a short persuasive paragraph on the topic *Reading is good for you.*
   b Write a short descriptive paragraph in which a character discovers something hidden away at the bottom of their garden. Aim to use:

   - a rhetorical question
   - repetition
   - pattern of three

   at least once in both paragraphs.

IMPROVING YOUR LEVEL

Level 3	Level 4	Level 5	Level 6
Occasionally use rhetorical devices, eg rhetorical questions	Sometimes use rhetorical devices, eg rhetorical questions, pattern of three	Use a range of rhetorical devices, eg rhetorical questions, pattern of three, repetition	Choose from a range of rhetorical devices, eg rhetorical questions, pattern of three, repetition, considering their effect on the reader

REMEMBER

- You can use rhetorical devices in your creative as well as your persuasive writing.
- Select rhetorical devices for their *effect* on the reader.
- Beware of using too many rhetorical devices.

5.4 Standard English and register

What am I learning?

You are learning to adapt the register of your writing depending on your audience.

We adapt the *register* of the language we use depending on our audience. Would you use the same words, or the same grammatical rules, when talking to your friends and writing a formal letter?

Look at some examples of spoken and written English.

> So I goes to him, I ain't never had a proper job before but I done other stuff for my dad and that. I would of asked for more money, but...

Ⓐ

Ⓑ

Dear Sir

I am writing to apply for the part-time job which I saw advertised in the local paper. Although this would be my first paid job, I have often worked for my father during the holidays.

1 What differences can you see in the language of the two examples?

2 What might be the effect if example B was written in the same *register* as example A?

3 Standard English is a version or *dialect* of English used in formal communication. For example, it is the language used to write:

- newspapers and television news bulletins
- formal letters, such as job applications
- non-fiction books such as biographies
- school text books
- information leaflets
- political speeches.

Why do you think this is?

Develop your understanding of standard English.

1 There are several differences between standard and non-standard English. For example:

Double negative

> I'm not eating nothing.

This sentence contains two negatives: 'not' and 'nothing'. Only one is needed. If two are used, one cancels out the other.

There are two ways of re-writing the non-standard English sentence above using standard English. What are they?

Verb agreement

2 In standard English, verb forms change depending on whether they are in the first, second or third person, singular or plural. For example, with the verb 'to be':

	Present tense		Past tense	
	singular	plural	singular	plural
1st person	I am	we are	I was	we were
2nd person	you are	you are	you were	you were
3rd person	he/she/it is	they are	he was	they were

Copy and complete the table for the verb to go and to have.

3 In non-standard English, the verb form does not always change in this way:

- You **was** supposed to be home by seven o'clock.
- I **was** home by half past seven.
- We **was** playing football till seven o'clock.

Re-write these non-standard English sentences using standard English.

Verb forms in the past tense

4 In standard English, some verbs have two different forms in the past tense:

> I **wrote** an email yesterday. I have **written** lots of emails today.

Sometimes, in non-standard English, only one verb form is used in the past tense:

> I ate my dinner yesterday. I've ate my dinner every night this week.

a Re-write the non-standard English sentence above using standard English.

b Re-write these sentences, changing the circled words into their standard English form:

  i I've done my homework. I done it earlier.

  ii I knew him when I was six. I've knew him all my life.

  iii I fell off my bike. I've fell off it loads of times.

Choose an appropriate register for your writing.

ACTIVITY 3

1 Look at these sentences:

  i r u goin 2 footie later

  ii I should not have took a note off my friend and read a note in your lesson.

  iii We are particularly concerned that this is not the first incident this term in which he has been involved.

  iv I promise this won't never happen again.

  v meet u in the hall at break

  vi I would be very grateful if you was able to discuss this matter with your son.

They are taken from a range of texts:

A a note passed from one student to another during a geography lesson

B an apology letter from the student to his geography teacher

C a letter from the head teacher to the student's parents.

2 a Which sentences come from which text?
  b Which is the most formal text? Which is the least formal text?
  c Are all the texts written using an appropriate register?
  d Can you identify any examples of non-standard English when standard English should have been chosen?

Use standard and non-standard English.

1 You witnessed the above 'incident' in which a student was caught passing a note.

  a Write down what you would tell your friends about the incident using non-standard English.
  b Your teacher has asked you to write a report, describing the incident you witnessed. Write the report using formal, standard English.

IMPROVING YOUR LEVEL

Level 3	Level 4	Level 5	Level 6
Sometimes uses non-standard English in formal writing	Occasionally uses non-standard English in formal writing	Usually use an appropriate register, depending on the audience	Always choose an appropriate register, depending on the task and its audience

REMEMBER

- Standard English is an important part of formal writing.
- Think about your audience and your register in all your writing.

AF5 Sample Answers: Levels 3-6

SENTENCES

The text

The Note
A friend tells you that they have found this scrap of paper in the street.

The question

1 Identify the key words in the question: purpose and form.

Write approximately 300 to 500 words, telling the story of what happened next. Aim to make your story imaginative and entertaining.

Use these questions to help you plan your story:
- What do you think the scrap of paper is?
- What does the X on the scrap of paper mean?
- What do you decide to do about it?

2 Identify the Assessment Focus which the question is assessing. Almost any writing task can be assessed on its sentence variety.

Writing Assessment Focus 5:

Vary sentences for clarity, purpose and effect by:
- using a range of sentence lengths and types for effect
- using sentence structures appropriate to your audience and the effect you want to create.

Level 3

- I usually write in simple sentences.
- I often use connectives like 'and', 'but' and 'so'.
- I sometimes use different tenses but not always consistently.

'It's a map. I bet it shows where someone has buried some treasure. Let's dig it up.' 'Don't be stupid,' said my friend. 'Why would someone do that?'
Anyway we was going home and I decided to get a spade and go to the park when it's dark and dig where the map says. So I go home. I eat my tea and got a spade out of the shed.

Mainly simple and compound sentences.

Moves from past to present tense and back again.

Non-standard English

Level 4

- I try to use a range of different lengths and types of sentences in my writing.
- I use a range of connectives in complex sentences, such as 'if', 'when', 'because', etc.
- I can use a range of different tenses, usually correctly and consistently.

It was getting dark when I arrived at the park. There was a group of children leaving as I arrived. They looked at me carrying a spade and laughed. I looked at the map and walked to the pond because that was where the 'X' was on the map. I began to dig. Then I saw the park keeper and I hid in a bush. Luckily he did not see me. I carried on digging. Suddenly my spade hits something hard.

A range of sentence types:
- **complex**
- **compound**
- **simple.**

Occasional inconsistent change of tense: from past to present.

A limited range of connectives.

Level 5

- I use a range of different lengths and types of sentences for effect.
- The range of connectives I use to link ideas in and between sentences is growing, for example, 'although', 'on the other hand', 'meanwhile', etc.
- I sometimes decide on the order in which I will write the words in a sentence to emphasise a detail or an idea.

Although my legs and arms were aching, I carried on digging until the hole was nearly half a metre deep. What would I find? That was what made me keep me going.

I kept digging even though I found nothing except an old can and a lot of other litter.

I was so busy digging that I did not see the light in the distance coming nearer, or hear the sound of footsteps, or the rattle of a bunch of keys, until it was too late and I felt a hand on my shoulder. I froze.

> Wider range of connectives used.

> A range of sentence types and lengths

> Long sentence structured to build tension to a surprise followed by a short sentence for dramatic effect.

> Rhetorical question to build tension and draw the reader in.

Level 6

- I can use a range of different lengths and types of sentence to achieve different effects, depending on the purpose of my writing.
- I often select the word order and structure of a sentence to achieve a particular effect.

I put down the spade and shone my torch into the hole. Beneath my feet, beneath a thin layer of soil was what looked like a square of dark, splintered wood and, attached to it, a rusting iron ring. It was a door.

It was then that I noticed the tapping noise. It was coming from beneath my feet. It was coming from the door.

> Long sentences structured to gradually reveal clues followed by short sentence used to add impact to the revelation.

> Series of short sentences using repetition to emphasise growing tension.

6.1 Commas

What am I learning?

You are learning to use commas to separate lists and clauses.

Like all punctuation, the comma helps writing make sense. It divides words, phrases and clauses, to show a short pause or break.

Look at the use of commas in lists.

You can use commas to separate items in a list. For example:

I went to the shops to buy chocolate, crisps, a drink and some carrots.

Notice that the last item in the list is linked using 'and' but no comma.

1 Look at the sentence below. It contains a list but the commas have been missed out.

He went into the kitchen. He got out the white bread brown bread French bread bread knife butter. He started to make the sandwiches.

  a Copy the sentence, adding commas and an 'and' to make its meaning clearer.
  b How many different items are there in the list?
  c How many commas did you need to add to make the meaning clearer?
  d Complete questions a–c again on the sentence at the top of the next page.

She went into the bathroom. There was a bath mat a bath bubble bath bath oil a bath robe a bath plug.

As well as items in a list, you can use commas to separate a list of actions or events. For example:

I went to the park, met my friends, played football and had an ice cream.

Notice again that the last event in the list is linked using 'and' without a comma.

2 Look at the sentence below. It contains a list of events but the commas have been missed out.

I got on my bike biked to the shops shopped until I dropped dropped my shopping off at home went out again.

   a Copy the sentence, adding commas and an 'and' to make its meaning clearer.
   b How many different events are there in the list?
   c How many commas did you need to add to make the meaning clearer?

Develop your use of commas to separate clauses.

1 Read the following sentences:

> I sold my bike on an auction website. My bike was 10 years old.

You can link both pieces of information together, writing them in just one sentence.

> I sold my bike, <u>which was 10 years old,</u> on an auction website.

...by adding this *relative clause*.

a What job are the two commas doing on either side of the relative clause?

b Look at the pairs of sentences below. Combine each pair into a single sentence with a relative clause, using linking words like:

who   which   whose   where

i My friend moved to Australia. My friend's name is Anwar.
ii My house has three bedrooms. My house is on Elm Avenue.
iii My dad has got a new job. My dad is 37 years old.

Choose when to use commas.

The relative clauses in the previous examples add extra information. In the examples below, the relative clauses do not add **extra** information...

> The student <u>who works the hardest</u> will win a prize.

> The classroom <u>in which my form is registered</u> is on the top floor.

...they add **essential** information. Without it, the main point of information in the sentence is lost.

1 Which of the relative clauses in the sentences below add extra information and which add essential information? Copy out the sentences, adding commas where they are needed.

a Bananas which are my favourite fruit are very good for you.
b The town where I used to live is five miles away.
c The boy who threw the paper plane will be punished.

You should also use commas to separate the clauses in some complex sentences. Complex sentences have two or more parts or clauses: a main clause and a subordinate clause. The subordinate clause adds more information, linked with a connective. For example:

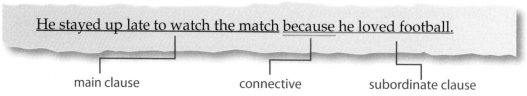

He stayed up late to watch the match because he loved football.

main clause   connective   subordinate clause

The two clauses can usually be swapped around without changing the sentence's meaning:

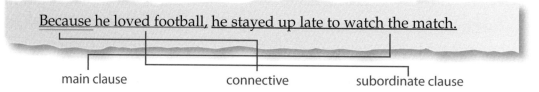

Because he loved football, he stayed up late to watch the match.

main clause   connective   subordinate clause

When the subordinate clause comes first in the sentence, you should use a comma to show where it finishes and the main clause begins.

2 Look at these complex sentences. Some start with a subordinate clause; some start with a main clause. Re-write them all so that they start with the subordinate clause, adding the comma in the correct place.

a When I was five I went to school.
b I soon settled in although I did not like it at first.
c I liked my teacher because she was kind.
d If I worked hard she gave me a gold star.

Use commas correctly.

ACTIVITY 4

1 Complete the following tasks, checking carefully that you are using commas correctly.

a Write a sentence which lists the members of your family.

In my family there is...

b   Write a sentence which lists things you did as a child.

When I was little I used to...

c   Write a sentence containing a relative clause about each of the following:

- your primary school
- your favourite holiday
- your favourite Christmas present

d   Write four complex sentences about your secondary school.

e   For each sentence, write an explanation of why you put commas where you did. Use the remember box below to help you.

IMPROVING YOUR LEVEL

Level 3	Level 4	Level 5	Level 6
Sometimes use commas in lists	Uses commas in lists and sometimes to separate clauses	Use commas in lists and to separate clauses but sometimes forget in longer more complicated sentences	Use commas accurately in subordinate and relative clauses with only occasional mistakes in longer more complicated sentences

REMEMBER

You should use commas:

- to separate items or actions in a list
- to separate a relative clause from the rest of the sentence
- to separate the subordinate clause at the start of the sentence.

6.2 Coming to a full stop

What am I learning?

You are learning how to use full stops to mark the end of your sentences.

We use sentences, marked with punctuation, to make communication clear and easy to understand. There are three different ways to end a sentence: with a full stop, a question mark or an exclamation mark.

Look at some sentences.

ACTIVITY 1

1 a Some of these are sentences, some are parts of a sentence and some are neither. Which is which?

- He sang as loudly as he could.
- Sausage you footballs be luckily better.
- Although no one really wanted to.
- Suddenly she started to run.
- When I was much younger.
- Did blue your by six river?

b All of these have been printed with a capital letter and a full stop or question mark, but it does not make all of them sentences. What do you think a *sentence* is? Write a short definition beginning 'A sentence is...'.

You can join two sentences into one sentence using a connective. For example, you can turn:

> He put on his boots. He ran onto the pitch.

> He put on his boots̶and H̶e ran onto the pitch.

2 a Look at these sentences:

- He tried the shoes on.
- He liked the shoes.
- It was getting dark.
- He decided to buy them.
- They were too expensive.
- He decided to go home.

b Use the connectives **and, but, so** to turn these six sentences into three sentences. Remember to put a full stop at the end of each one.

Develop your use of full stops.

ACTIVITY 2

Sentences are made up of chunks of information or clauses. For example:

I went to visit my Grandma.

This is a clause

I knocked on the door

This is a clause

and went in.

and so is this.

I was a bit suspicious

This is a clause

because she had such big teeth.

and so is this.

1 a How many pieces of information or clauses can you find in this writing?

Little Red Riding Hood jumped up it was not Grandma in the bed it was the wolf she tried to run to the door the wolf was too quick for her he grabbed her suddenly the door burst open a woodcutter came running in he had an axe the woodcutter killed the wolf they heard someone knocking someone was shut in the cupboard they opened the cupboard Grandma climbed out

b Copy out the story of Little Red Riding Hood above, putting a full stop at the end of each clause.

c Choose six clauses from the story then re-write them as three longer sentences using the connectives 'and', 'but' and 'so'.

Choose when to use full stops, commas and connectives.

You can either join two clauses with a connective or separate them with a full stop. You should **not** use a comma to separate them if you are **not** using a connective (unless you are listing events or actions – see pages 121 and 122).

Correct: | She tasted the big bowl of porridge but it was too hot. ✓

connective

Incorrect: | She sat on the tiny chair, it was just right. ✗

no connective here

> Remember if you do not use a connective to join two clauses, they should be in separate sentences, separated with a full stop (or a question mark, or an exclamation mark).

1 Now look at these sentences:

   a She went upstairs and saw three beds.
   b She lay down on the first bed, it was too hard.
   c She tried the second bed but it was too soft.
   d She tried the third bed, she went straight to sleep.

   Which ones are correctly punctuated? Re-write those which are not, correcting them by removing the comma and adding a connective.

2 Look at the clauses below. Use them to write the opening of a ghost story. Use connectives to combine some, and leave some as short, simple sentences. Remember to use a full stop at the end of each sentence.

the house was built at the end of a long, dark lane

there were no curtains in the windows

the sun hardly ever shone on the house

some of the windows had been boarded up

no one lived there

> Some connectives you could use include:
> • and
> • but
> • so
> • when
> • although
> • because
> • since.

the last occupants left over 30 years ago

some people said they had seen a young girl's face at the window

even in summer the air was cold there

Use full stops correctly.

1 a Write six or seven sentences about 'The Happiest Day of My Life So Far'.
  b Make sure you have used full stops correctly.
  c Copy your sentences onto a piece of paper but **leave out** all the full stops.
  d Swap your writing with a partner.
  e Correct your partner's writing by adding full stops.
  f Check your work against your partner's. Do you agree on the right places for the full stops?

IMPROVING YOUR LEVEL

Level 3	Level 4	Level 5	Level 6
Use some full stops	Usually use full stops correctly, sometimes using commas instead	Always use full stops correctly	Choose whether to use a full stop or a connective depending on the intended effect on the reader

REMEMBER

- Full stops help your writing make sense.
- Join clauses with connectives, not commas.
- Every time you write a comma, check whether it should be a full stop.

6.3 Apostrophes

What am I learning?

You are learning how to use apostrophes of omission and apostrophes of ownership.

Apostrophes can be used to show that letters have been missed out of a word and to show that something belongs to someone.

Why we use an apostrophe to show ownership

In Old English, spoken and written around 1000 years ago, they showed something belonged to someone by adding -es to the word. For example, *Alfredes axe* meant the axe belonging to Alfred. In modern English, we would write: Alfred's axe. We leave out the 'e' and use an apostrophe to show it's been missed out.

Look at some examples of apostrophes of omission.

ACTIVITY 1

Omission

You can use an apostrophe to create *contractions* – two words squashed into one – when you are writing informally. The apostrophe shows where one or more letters has been missed out. **Note that it is not used to show that the space between the two words is missing.** For example:

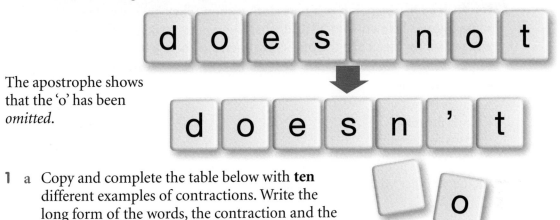

The apostrophe shows that the 'o' has been *omitted*.

1 a Copy and complete the table below with **ten** different examples of contractions. Write the long form of the words, the contraction and the missing letters indicated by the apostrophe.

Long form	Contraction	Missing letters
does not did not	doesn't	o
	he's	

b Write a playscript or a cartoon of a conversation between a parent and a teenager, like the one opposite. Try to use as many different contractions as you can. Remember to check you are using apostrophes correctly.

Develop your use of apostrophes to show ownership.

 ACTIVITY 2

To show that something belongs to someone, you will need one of these: **'**

and, usually, one of these: **s**

For example:

The **pencil** belonging to **Rhiannon** is **Rhiannon's pencil**.

1 Complete these examples:

This	Belongs to	It's
pencil ruler pen book	Rhiannon Laura Sohan Dan	Rhiannon's pencil

If the owner's name ends in -s, you do not need to add an extra one. You just add the apostrophe. For example:

The **cat** belonging to **Jess** is **Jess'** cat.

no extra 's'

2 You've got a Saturday job in a new clothes shop. They have asked you to write some signs to help customers find what they want. Write out the words you will put on the signs like the one shown here, to show where customers can find:

- shoes for boys
- shoes for girls
- suits for men
- jeans for women.

children's clothing

Remember to put the ['] in the correct place – and decide whether you need to add an extra [S].

Choose the right spelling for homophones with apostrophes.

ACTIVITY 3

Some words sound the same but have different spellings to show they have different meanings. For example:

your = belonging to you   you're = contraction of 'you are'

its = belonging to it   it's = contraction of 'it is'

their = belonging to them   there = indicating place,   they're = contraction
                               e.g. over there   of 'they are'

To work out whether the spelling with the apostrophe is correct, separate the contraction back into two words. So, this sentence:

> They're walking into town later.

still makes sense when you separate

(they're)   into   (they)   and   (are)

1 Which of these sentences are correctly spelt? Copy and correct them.

 a When they get their, there going to do some shopping.
 b Its a well known fact that boy's never tidy there rooms.
 c Your going to lose your money if you don't look after it.
 d Its time for the dog to have its dinner.
 e Have you lost you're phone? Its on the floor over their.

Use apostrophes correctly.

ACTIVITY 4

These three students have got their PE kit all mixed up.

1 a Who has got whose shirt? Write your answer in complete sentences. For example you might think that:

> Meena has got Joe's shirt.

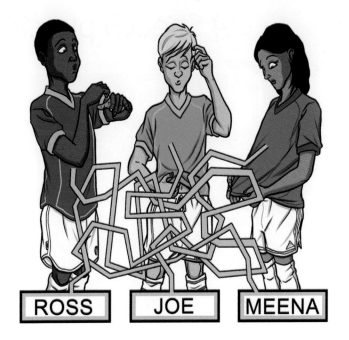

ROSS   JOE   MEENA

Remember to use apostrophes correctly.

b Complete these sentences using the correct homophone.

There	_____PE kit is all mixed up.
Their	_____ trying to sort it out.
They're	_____are three lost shirts.
Its	___ easy to find your kit if ___ labelled.
It's	My shirt has lost ___ labels.
You're	_____ PE kit should be clearly labelled.
Your	_____ likely to get a detention if you lose your kit.

IMPROVING YOUR LEVEL

Level 3	Level 4	Level 5	Level 6
Sometimes use apostrophes in contractions but not always in the right place	Sometimes use apostrophes in contractions and to show possession	Usually use apostrophes correctly in contractions and to show possession	Always use apostrophes correctly, including homophones

REMEMBER

- Apostrophes show where letters have been missed out in a contraction.
- Apostrophes show ownership.
- If the owner's name ends in -s, there is no need to add an 's' after the apostrophe.

6.4 Speech punctuation

What am I learning?
You are learning how to use speech punctuation correctly.

When you write a story you will almost certainly want to include dialogue: the characters talking to each other using direct speech. To make your meaning clear, you need to use speech punctuation accurately. This means not only using speech marks correctly, but a range of other punctuation as well.

Look at the punctuation in some dialogue.

ACTIVITY 1

1 Read this extract from the novel *Somewhere Else* by Sandra Glover. A girl has woken up in a house which she is sure is not her own, but everyone who lives there seems to know her.

> 'Hey,' said the boy. 'What's wrong? Why're you lookin' at me like that?'
>
> 'Who are you?' she asked.
>
> 'Duh!' said the boy. 'Zan. Alexander. Your brother?' he said, emphasising each word.
>
> 'I haven't got a brother.' She knew that. She didn't know how she knew but she did. Sisters, she had older sisters, two of them. What were their names?
>
> 'You wish!' the boy was saying. 'Hey Jade, what is it, what's wrong?'

2 Make a list of all the punctuation which the writer has used to punctuate this dialogue.

Develop your use of speech punctuation.

1 Look again at the extract and use it to answer the questions below.

a What do speech marks ' ' tell the reader?

b When should you use a punctuation mark immediately **after** closing speech marks?

c Which punctuation marks can you use immediately **before** closing speech marks?

2 Compare these two pieces of dialogue from the extract.

'Hey,' said the boy.

'I haven't got a brother.' She knew that. She didn't know how she knew but she did.

'Who are you?' she asked.

a Why is there a comma **before** the closing speech marks here?

b Why is there a full stop **before** the closing speech marks here?

c Why does this word **after** the closing speech marks begin with a small letter?

d Why does this word **after** the closing speech marks begin with a capital letter?

e Why is it surprising that this word begins with a small letter?

4 Use your answers to questions 1 and 2 to help you write *A Guide to Speech Punctuation*.

Use these questions to help you:

- How do you show which words are spoken by a character?
- When do you put a punctuation mark **straight after** closing speech marks?
- When do you use a comma **before** the closing speech marks?
- When do you use a full stop **before** the closing speech marks?
- When do you use a small letter for the word **after** the closing speech marks?
- When do you use a capital letter for the word **after** the closing speech marks?

Choose the right speech punctuation.

1 Look at the story below. All the speech punctuation has been missed out. Copy out the dialogue, adding a piece of punctuation every time you see one of these _.

A man went to a flying school.
_ I want to learn to fly_ _ he said.
_ You want to learn today_ _ said the instructor.
_ Yes please_ _ said the man.
_ We're very busy today_ _ said the instructor. _ I haven't got any planes spare_ _
_ It has to be today_ _ said the man. _ I'll pay ten thousand pounds_ _
_ I tell you what_ _ said the instructor_ _ I'll teach you how to fly that helicopter. You can fly it solo and I'll stay down here and tell you how to do it over the radio. OK_ _
_ Fine._
The instructor showed the man how to start the helicopter, explained the basics and sent him on his way.
After he climbed to 1000 feet, the man radioed in.
_ This isn't too difficult_ _ he said. _ And the view's amazing_ _
Once the man reached 2000 feet, he radioed in again.
_ This is easy_ _ he cried.
The instructor watched him climb to 3000 feet and began to worry that the man hadn't radioed in. Suddenly the helicopter plummeted to the ground and crashed. The instructor ran over and pulled the man from the wreckage.
_ What happened_ _ asked the instructor.
_ It was all going so well_ _ said the man. But then I got cold and turned off the big fan_ _

2 Using each of the fridge magnets below, make as many different, accurately punctuated lines of dialogue as you can.

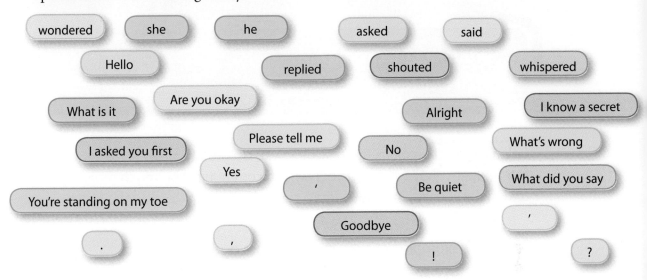

Use a range of speech punctuation accurately.

Your teacher has said that you must stay in at lunch time to complete your homework. Write down the conversation in which you try to persuade your teacher to let you off – and your teacher refuses. Aim to:

- write approximately ten lines of dialogue
- use a range of different punctuation marks including commas, full stops, exclamation and question marks.

IMPROVING YOUR LEVEL

Level 3	Level 4	Level 5	Level 6
Sometimes uses speech marks	Usually uses speech marks	Always uses speech marks and usually some other speech punctuation but not always accurately	Always use speech marks and other speech punctuation accurately

REMEMBER

- Speech marks show the reader what a character says.
- There is **always** a punctuation mark before the closing speech marks.
- Think carefully whether the word after the closing speech marks should have a capital letter.

6.5 Colons and semi-colons

What am I learning?

You are learning how to use colons and semi-colons accurately.

Colons and semi-colons are difficult to use accurately. However, if you can master them, they will make your written communication **much** more precise and make your writing **much** more sophisticated.

Look at examples of how to use colons and semi-colons.

ACTIVITY 1

You can use a colon to introduce a list:

> You will need: eggs, flour, sugar and margarine.

You can also use a colon to introduce an example – like this one.

1   a   You are writing a recipe for a cheese sandwich. Begin by explaining the ingredients you will need, using a colon and some commas.
    b   How many people do you live with? What are their names? Write a sentence beginning:

The people I live with…

Use a colon and some commas to introduce and list their names.

If the list you are writing is a list of phrases rather than single words, you can use a semi-colon to separate them instead of commas. It makes your list much easier to understand. For example:

colon to introduce list

> On my holiday, I went to: a theme park in England; an activity centre in Scotland; and a horse-riding centre in Wales.

semi-colon to separate listed items

2 a What are your three favourite things? Why? Write a sentence, beginning:

> My favourite three things are…

b Then list each favourite thing and the reason why you love it, for example:

> … my dog because he's fun and cuddly.

Use a colon to introduce your list and semi-colons to separate each item.

Develop your use of the semi-colon.

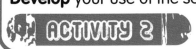

You can also use semi-colons in sentences to link two clauses. For example:

> I eat a jar of pickled onions every day because I love them.

connective used to link the two clauses

could be written as:

> I eat a jar of pickled onions every day; I love them.

semi-colon to separate and link clauses

1 a Look at the pairs of sentences below.

a. My feet hurt.	My shoes are too tight.
b. I went to the swimming pool.	It was closed.
c. I walked home in the rain.	I got soaked.
d. I love using semi-colons.	They're so easy!

b Re-write each pair as a single sentence:

- first linked with a connective
- then replacing the connective with a semi-colon.

Choose: full stop, semi-colon or colon?

You can see if you are using semi-colons correctly by checking that:

- the two halves are closely related
- the two halves of the sentence make clear sense and can stand alone.
  For example:

> I love apples; tomatoes are good for you.

Both halves of the sentence above make sense by themselves, but they're not very closely related. They should be written as two sentences, separated by a full stop.

> I love apples; they're healthy, crunchy and delicious.

Both halves of this sentence are related and make sense by themselves:

> I love apples | they're healthy, crunchy and delicious.

The second half of the sentence below doesn't make sense without the first half.

> I love apples; <u>healthy, crunchy and delicious.</u>

But it **is** an explanation, so you can introduce it with a colon:

> I love apples: healthy, crunchy and delicious.

1 Which punctuation mark should separate these pairs?

a My auntie lives in Doncaster   her house is near the train station.
b My grandad lives in London   the biggest city in the UK.
c My auntie lives in Doncaster   my granddad loves football.
d I visited her last summer   it was the best holiday ever.
e London's great   noisy and dirty, but full of things to see and do.
f London's huge   Doncaster is in Yorkshire.

Use colons and semi-colons accurately.

Look at the text below. It is taken from a guide for adults on how to use and enjoy email.

Sequence and punctuate the instructions using colons, semi-colons or connectives.

| To use and enjoy email, you will need | a computer with an email program such as Thunderbird or Outlook | an Internet connection | a friend to email. |

Email is quick and easy — it takes a few seconds to write and even less time to arrive.

You can send as many emails as you like — once you've paid for your Internet connection, it's completely free.

You can use email to — write to your friends, send photos and news to your family, and contact businesses.

Don't be frustrated if you find it difficult at first — emailing gets easier with practice.

IMPROVING YOUR LEVEL

Level 3	Level 4	Level 5	Level 6
I never use colons or semi colons	Occasionally uses colons	Occasionally uses colons and semi colons though not always accurately	Uses colons with confidence and semi colons with some accuracy

REMEMBER

- You can use a colon to introduce a list or an example.
- You can use semi-colons to separate phrases in a list.
- You can use semi-colons to link related clauses in a sentence, instead of a connective.

AF6 Sample Answers: Levels 3–6

PUNCTUATION

The question

> 1 Identify the key words in the question: audience, purpose and form.

Write a short story for teenagers. Choose one of the titles below:
- **Missing**
- **The Mistake**

Aim to:
- write 200 to 300 words
- describe characters and settings
- write accurately and clearly.

> 2 Identify the Assessment Focus which the question is assessing.

Writing Assessment Focus 6:

Write with technical accuracy of syntax and punctuation by:
- using full stops, question and exclamation marks to mark the end of a sentence
- using commas, colons and semi-colons in lists and to mark or separate clauses
- using a range of punctuation accurately in speech.

Level 3

- I sometimes use full stops, capital letters, question and exclamation marks accurately to show where my sentences start and finish.
- Sometimes I use commas to join sentences when I should use full stops to separate them.
- I can use speech marks but sometimes I forget.

> A man and woman were in their House watching the TV when they realised their son should have been Home by now.
> 'where is he' asked the woman
> I don't know said the man.
> The woman whose name was Lucy went out to look in the street, she couldnt see Him anywhere, He had gone missing.

Some capital letters at the start of sentences...

... some capital letters incorrectly used in the middle of sentences.

Commas used to join sentences – should be full stops.

Missing apostrophe

Speech marks used correctly here... ...but not here.

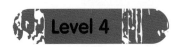

Level 4

- I always use full stops, questions marks and exclamation marks accurately.
- I use speech marks accurately. Sometimes I use other punctuation inside the speech marks but I am not always sure when it is correct.
- I use commas in lists. I sometimes use commas in complex sentences but I am not always sure when they are correct.

> She couldn't find it anywhere. She looked in the bedroom, in the front room, in the kitchen and in the bathroom. It was nowhere to be found.
> Later that day her husband came home.
> 'I can't find that ring you bought me.' she said. 'I've looked everywhere but I can't find it. Have you seen it?'
> 'You could'nt have lost it,' said her husband.
> Although she had looked everywhere already they began to look again.

Full stop and question marks used correctly.

Commas used correctly to separate list of events.

Speech marks used correctly.

Subordinate clause in complex sentence should have a comma at end.

Apostrophe used but misplaced.

Incorrect full stop inside speech marks – should be a comma.

143

Level 5

- I use full stops, question marks, exclamation marks and speech punctuation accurately.
- Readers usually find it easy to understand my sentences because of the word order and punctuation I choose.
- I am often unsure where to put commas in longer, more complicated sentences.

'I cant believe youve done this to me,' Ellie screamed.
'Done what?' asked Ellies mum. 'It was you that lied to me,' her mum said quietly walking towards the door, and closing it, quietly so that her dad who was in the other room, could not hear them. Ellie sat down at the kitchen table with her head in her hands. She began to cry quietly. Why was her mum doing this to her?
'I've already told you. I didn't lie to you. It's all a mistake. And I'm going to prove it.'

Missing apostrophes of contraction and ownership.

Speech marks used correctly.

Full stops and question marks used accurately.

Commas misplaced in long, complex sentence. This does not help clear communication.

Accurate punctuation used inside speech marks.

Level 6

- Readers always find it easy to understand my sentences because of the word order I choose and the accuracy of my punctuation.
- I am occasionally unsure where to put commas in longer, more complicated sentences.

He sat alone in the cold, dark police cell wondering, if he would be behind bars for the rest of his life.
Did they really suspect him of such a terrible crime? Of course they did; they had arrested him.
'Someone to see you,' said a voice.
'Who?' he mumbled.
'It's me,' said a woman's voice. The cell door groaned on its hinges. 'Nice place you've got here.'

Comma misplaced in long, complex sentence.

Full stops and question marks used accurately.

Correct use of semi-colon.

Correct use of apostrophes.

Speech marks used correctly.
A range of punctuation used correctly inside speech punctuation.

AF7 VOCABULARY

7.1 Word choice

> **What am I learning?**
>
> You are learning to select the best words in your writing, thinking about their effect.

explicit meaning: the clearly and definitely expressed meaning

implicit meaning: indirectly suggested, a hidden meaning

For example, when a teacher says, 'Do you want a detention?', what they are implying – what they mean but are not actually saying – is 'Behave!'

Writers choose words not only because they make sense, but also because of the ideas that they suggest. The writer's choice of language can influence the reader's opinion; create a picture in the reader's mind; suggest an extra layer of **implicit** meaning beneath the obvious, **explicit** meaning; or all three.

Look at three newspaper headlines.

1 Look at the headlines on the next page. They all appeared on the same day, following the publication of the results of an opinion poll. The poll asked a selection of adults in the UK which political party they would vote for if there were a general election the next day.

Voting intentions …

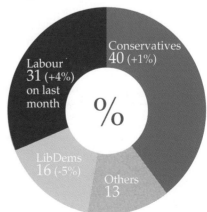

Conservatives 40 (+1%)

Labour 31 (+4%) on last month

LibDems 16 (-5%)

Others 13

%

A Labour government slash Tory opinion poll lead

B TORIES' LEAD OVER LABOUR SHRINKS TO SINGLE FIGURES

C LABOUR CLOSING GAP ON CONSERVATIVES

> **biased:** prejudiced, favouring one side over another

a Which headline is the most **biased**, written to appeal to Labour Party supporters?

b Which headline is the least biased, written to appeal to neither Labour nor Conservative Party supporters?

Develop your awareness of language choice.

ACTIVITY 2

1 Look closely at the above headlines, particularly the language which the headline writers have chosen to use to describe the change in the opinion poll.

a The writer of headline A uses the word 'slash'. Write down all the ideas and thoughts that this word suggests to you. You could record them on a spidergram like the one below.

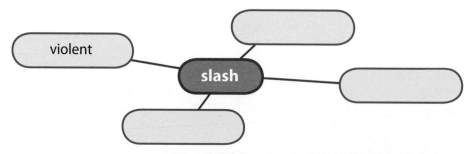

violent — slash

b The writer of headline B uses the word 'shrinks'. Write down all the ideas and thoughts that this word suggests to you. You could record them on a spidergram like the one below.

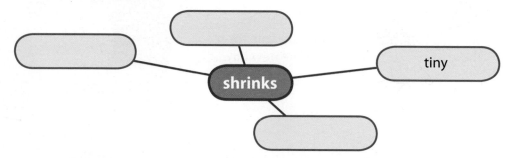

shrinks — tiny

c Which choice of word suggests the most dramatic change in the popularity of the two political parties?

Choose vocabulary for its **connotations** and effect.

> **synonym:** a word with the same or a similar meaning to another word
>
> **connotation:** the ideas or feelings we associate with a particular word

1 Look at this extract from a thesaurus. It shows some of the different **synonyms** for the word 'smell'.

> **smell** (noun)
>
> | | |
> |---|---|
> | odour | stench |
> | aroma | stink |
> | fragrance | whiff |
> | scent | |

a Which word do you think has the **most positive** connotations?

b Which word do you think has the **most negative** connotations?

c Rank the remaining synonyms, from most to least positive.

d Choose one of the synonyms. Write a descriptive sentence in which you use your chosen synonym. What connotations does the word suggest to you? Record them on a spidergram.

e Choose another synonym which you feel has very different connotations. Write a descriptive sentence using your chosen synonym. What connotations does this synonym have? Record them on a spidergram.

2 a Look at this student's description of a visit to a safari park.

> The lions strutted around, looking lean and mean, feasting on hunks of meat.

b Using the extracts from a thesaurus on the next page, rewrite the sentences above to create a much less positive image of the lions.

strut *go*
lumber
march
pace
plod
prance
roam
shuffle
stride
traipse
tramp
trudge
wander

feast *bite*
chew
devour
dine
feed
munch
pick at
polish off
snack

meat *food*
flesh
grub
gristle

hunk *batch*
chunk
clump
lump
nugget
portion
slab

mean *bad-tempered*
dangerous
evil
hard
malicious
nasty
rough
troublesome
ugly
unfriendly
vicious
vile

lean *bony*
emaciated
gaunt
meagre
scrawny
skinny
slim
wasted

Use a wider vocabulary in your writing.

ACTIVITY 4

1 a Write four or five sentences describing your favourite place in the world. It could be a country, a town or a room.

  b Choose five descriptive words from your sentences. Write down five synonyms for each word, trying to include some with positive connotations and some with negative connotations.

  c Now re-write your four or five sentences, choosing vocabulary with negative connotations to describe the **same** place as if it were your **least** favourite in the world.

IMPROVING YOUR LEVEL

Level 3	Level 4	Level 5	Level 6
Chooses words for their explicit meaning; often repeats vocabulary	Sometimes chooses words for their effect	Often chooses words for their implied meaning, considering their effect on the reader, eg positive or negative associations	Always chooses words for their implied meaning and connotations beyond positive and negative associations

REMEMBER

- Think about the words you choose in your writing and the effect you want them to create.
- Descriptive vocabulary can have negative and positive connotations.
- Your choice of vocabulary can create a picture in the reader's mind and influence their opinion.

7.2 Rhetorical devices

What am I learning?

You are learning to use a range of rhetorical devices in your writing.

Writers use a number of language techniques or tricks in their writing to create an effect and influence the reader's response.

Look at a range of rhetorical devices.

> **contrast:** a noticeable difference between two things

1 Look at these extracts from 'The Farmer's Wife', a poem in which Jack the farmer discovers he has married a werewolf.

This is the beginning of the poem:

'Spring is the time for a wedding
And I'll be married in May
When the thorn is white and from
first light
The young lambs frolic and play,'
Said Jack, the farmer of Fairness
Watching the mountain side
And the high house where by her
glittering hair
He could see Julie Ann, his bride.

And this is the end of the poem, when Jack realises his wife is a werewolf and he must try to kill her:

O he has no silver bullets
And what are bullets of lead
To the werewolf there whose red
eyes stare
Under the light of the moon?

a How would you describe the mood or atmosphere at the start of the poem?
b How would you describe the mood or atmosphere at the end of the poem?
c Why do you think the writer has chosen to use these two **contrasting** moods?

2 Look at this extract from Shakespeare's *Macbeth*.
   Macbeth has killed the King and is now filled
   with guilt.

> **hyperbole:** intentional
> exaggeration

> MACBETH: Will all great Neptune's ocean wash this blood
>   Clean from my hand?

   a How much water does Macbeth think he will need to wash the blood from
      his hands?
   b What does this exaggeration, or *hyperbole*, suggest about the blood on
      Macbeth's hands and the guilt in Macbeth's mind?

3 Look at this extract from Seamus Heaney's
   translation of the Old English poem, *Beowulf*.
   The evil monster Grendel is about to attack the
   hero Beowulf and his men.

> **alliteration:** two or more
> words placed near to each
> other, beginning with the
> same letter or sound

> Then his rage boiled over, he ripped open
> the mouth of the building, maddening for blood,
> pacing the length of the patterned floor
> with his loathsome tread, while a baleful light,
> flame more than light, flared from his eyes.

   a Copy the extract, circling the alliterative
      words, for example,
   b What effect do you think the writer is trying
      to create in the extract?
   c How does the writer's use of **alliteration**
      contribute to this effect?

Develop your use of rhetorical devices.

ACTIVITY 2

Contrast

1 Look at these sentences:

> Eric was not enjoying the party. He sat alone in a
> corner, with his party hat pulled down over his
> eyes, picking at his birthday cake.

   a Identify the purpose of the text and the effect the writer is trying to achieve
   b Add a sentence or two, using contrast to emphasise the effect.
   c Write a sentence or two, commenting on the effect you have created using
      contrast.

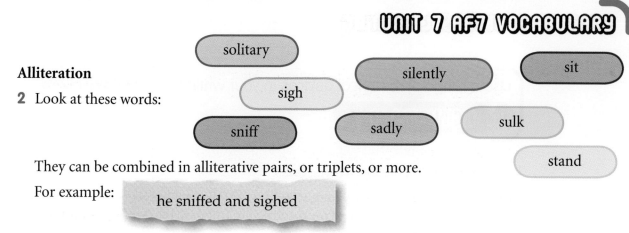

Alliteration

2 Look at these words:

They can be combined in alliterative pairs, or triplets, or more.

For example:

> he sniffed and sighed

Look again at question 1. Add another sentence or two to your writing, using alliteration to give emphasis and/or dramatic effect.

Hyperbole

3 a Look at these examples of hyperbole. Which are effective and which are so exaggerated that they spoil the overall effect of the writing?

> 'You left me at that horrible party for about three weeks,' sobbed Eric as his mother drove him home.

> 'Don't be upset, Eric. You're the sweetest, most adorable child in the world.'

> Eric howled so loudly that glass could be heard cracking in several of the neighbours' windows.

b What is the intended effect of the hyperbole in these examples?

Choose from a range of rhetorical devices for effect.

1 These sentences are from students' argument writing on the topic, 'School Detentions Should Be Banned'.

> Despite millions of detentions given over hundreds of years, students are still misbehaving.

> They are like a club for badly behaved students.

> While some students walk free in the fresh air, others are shut in a dark room against their will.

> Detentions mean nothing to the hardened offender, used to years of imprisonment.

> Detentions are where schools dump the disobedient and the disrespectful.

a Identify the rhetorical devices used in each one.

b Choose some of these – and add some of your own sentences – to write an effective introduction to the argument.

Use a range of rhetorical devices in your writing.

1 You are working on two writing tasks:
   - a story about an elderly man who lives in a derelict house
   - a speech persuading your local council to improve local facilities for teenagers.

   a In each case, how could you use contrast, alliteration and hyperbole in your writing?
   b Write a paragraph from each task, using a range of rhetorical devices for effect.

IMPROVING YOUR LEVEL

Level 3	Level 4	Level 5	Level 6
Occasionally use rhetorical devices, eg alliteration	Sometimes use rhetorical devices, eg alliteration, hyperbole	Use a range of rhetorical devices, eg alliteration, hyperbole, contrast	Choose from a range of rhetorical devices, eg alliteration, hyperbole, contrast, considering their effect on the reader

REMEMBER

- **Alliteration** can be used to create emphasis or drama in your writing.
- **Hyperbole** and contrast can be used to exaggerate a point.
- **Rhetorical devices** can be used in a range of different texts – not just argument or persuasion.

7.3 Figurative language

What am I learning?

You are learning to use figurative language to create a strong image in your reader's mind.

Figurative language uses imagery – an image drawn using words – to take the picture which is in the writer's head and put it into the reader's head.

Look at examples of simile and metaphor.

> **simile:** a comparison of two different things, using 'like' or 'as'

1 Look at these two similes:

> His eyes were like puddles of murky rainwater.

> His teeth were as blunt as boulders.

a In each one, identify:
- the *source* in the simile – what is being described
- the *target* in the simile – what it is being compared to.

b You can use a Venn diagram to help you explore the image a simile creates. The words in the central overlapping area describe what the *source* and the *target* might have in common:

Copy the Venn diagram, adding two more words to the centre.

c Draw a new Venn diagram to explore the image created in the second example above.

metaphor: a direct comparison of two different things, without the use of 'like' or 'as', suggesting a much stronger similarity

2 You can turn some similes into **metaphors** by removing the words 'like' or 'as'. For example:

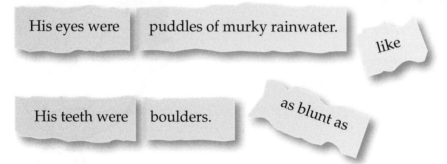

a Re-write these similes as metaphors:

- His nostrils were like dark caverns.
- His lips were as thin and brown as bread crusts.
- His chin was like a hammer head and every word he spoke was like a nail.

b Use these Venn diagrams to think of an effective simile to describe:

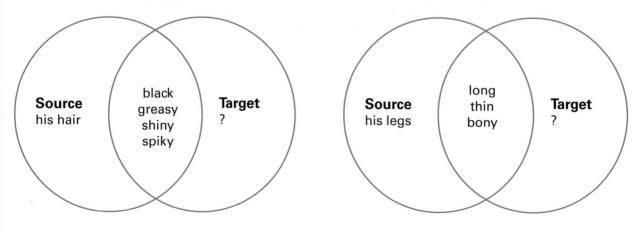

c Re-write the similes you created in question 2b as metaphors.

Develop your use of figurative language.

ACTIVITY 2

1 Some similes are so familiar to us that they have become clichés and so they no longer create a picture in our heads.

   a Complete these well-known similes:

- as cool as a...
- as green as...
- as white as...

- as cunning as...
- as quiet as...
- as strong as...

   b Now complete the similes in question 1a using **new** and **original** ideas.

2 Look at this example of personification:

> The wind screamed and shrieked.

> **personification:** a kind of metaphor, describing a non-human object as if it were a person

The wind does not actually 'scream' or 'shriek', but these human actions suggest human emotion to create an atmosphere of fear and terror.

   a Pair these non-human objects with these human activities to create five sentences which use personification. For example,

The leaves danced.

leaves	bellow	smile
trees	dance	sing
clouds	skip	sigh
the sun	run	plod
the wind	glare	whisper

   b Look again at your answers to question 2a. What human emotion is suggested by each of the examples of personification? What mood or atmosphere does it create?

Choose a variety of figurative language to create an effective description.

You have been asked to describe 'The most evil teacher in the world'. Look at one student's planning for the task:

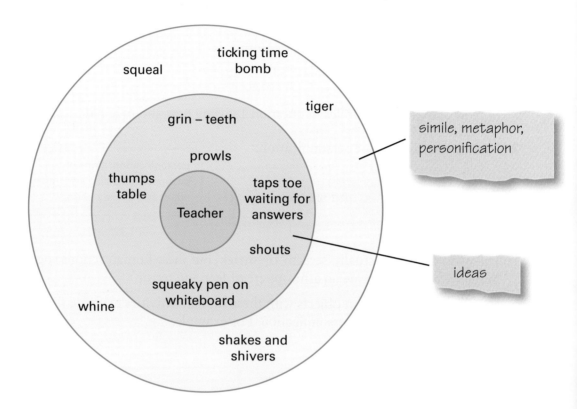

Use this planning and your own ideas to write four or five sentences, using a variety of simile, metaphor and personification.

Use a variety of figurative language.

Write a short description entitled 'My Perfect Classroom'. Aim to describe:

- the students
- the teacher
- the classroom
- the mood or atmosphere.

Try to use at least one simile, one metaphor and one piece of personification.

IMPROVING YOUR LEVEL

Level 3	Level 4	Level 5	Level 6
Occasionally uses similes in descriptive writing	Sometimes uses similes in descriptive writing, although sometimes uses cliches; uses metaphor occasionally	Often uses similes and metaphors in descriptive writing with growing originality; uses personification occasionally	Uses a range of figurative language with some originality, considering its effect on the reader

REMEMBER

- Simile, metaphor and personification can create an image in the reader's mind.
- Avoid clichés – use new and original figurative language.
- Try to use a variety of figurative language – but don't overuse it.

7.4 Using a dictionary and thesaurus

What am I learning?

You are learning to use a dictionary and thesaurus to improve the accuracy and breadth of your vocabulary choice.

Often in your writing you can rely on the vocabulary you carry around in your own head. Sometimes, though, you need a helping hand.

Look at an extract from a dictionary.

ACTIVITY 1

---

the origins of the word ──

help on how to pronounce the word ──

the entry word: the word you are looking up ──

── guide words to show which words are on these pages

sesame   **settle**

sesame (sess-a-mee) *noun*
the seeds from a tropical plant, used in bread, sweets and cakes or as a spice.
[Greek]

session (sesh-'n) *noun*
1 the meeting together of a court, group or organization.
2 any single meeting for a particular purpose: *The orchestra has two practice sessions weekly.*

set *verb*
1 to put: *Set the chairs around the table.*
2 to become hard or firm: *The ice cream set quickly in the freezer.*
3 to give a fixed position or shape to: *The gem was set in gold.*
4 to start: *His father set him up in business.*
5 (of the sun, moon, etc.) to sink below the horizon.

set *noun*
1 a number of things which together form a complete collection: *a set of dinner plates.*
2 the way in which something stands or is placed: *the determined set of his jaw.*

3 an apparatus which receives radio signals, etc.: *a television set.*
4 the scenery used to represent a particular place during a play or film.
5 a group of students of a similar ability in a particular subject who are taught together.
set *adjective* fixed: *Have you read the set texts?*

setback *noun*
a reverse or check to progress: *Farming suffered a setback during the drought.*

settee *noun*
a sofa.

setting *noun*
1 that in which something is set: *The play's setting was ancient Rome.*
2 the arrangement of cutlery, mats, glasses, etc.; on a table.

settle *verb*
1 to agree: *We finally settled on where to spend our holiday.*
2 to sink down or rest: *The mud settled on the river bottom.*

── the meaning or *definition* of the word

── part of speech: noun, verb, adverb, adjective, etc.

1 Using the dictionary extract opposite, write three different sentences using a different meaning of the *verb* 'set' in each one.

2 Now write three different sentences using a different meaning of the *noun* 'set' in each one.

3 What does the word 'settle' mean? Using the dictionary, write a definition **in your own words**.

4 Look at the extract opposite. The word 'setting' is listed before the word 'settle'. Write a few sentences for someone who has never used a dictionary before, explaining why this is.

5 The *guide words* appear at the top left and right corners of each double page. The first guide word is the first word on that page. The last guide word is the last word on that page.

The guide words below have been taken from different pages in the dictionary. Which of the words on the right will you find on which pages?

chemistry

48 check	chip 49

cheer

child

chuckle

class

cinema

claim

chest

cinder

52 chronicle	circular 53

chuck

cheetah

circumstance

circle

city

54 circulate	clause 55

citizen

clap

cheese

Develop your dictionary and thesaurus skills.

A thesaurus is a book which lists synonyms – words which have the same or similar meaning. For example, if you look up the word 'huge' in a thesaurus, it will give you these synonyms:

huge (adjective)	*humongous*
big	*immense*
bulky	*large*
capacious	*massive*
colossal	*mountainous*
copious	*sizable*
enormous	*spacious*
fat	*substantial*
gigantic	*vast*
great	*whopping*
huge	

However you can also use a thesaurus to look up a spelling – because it can be difficult to find a word in the dictionary when you don't know how to spell it.

1 a Look at these words:

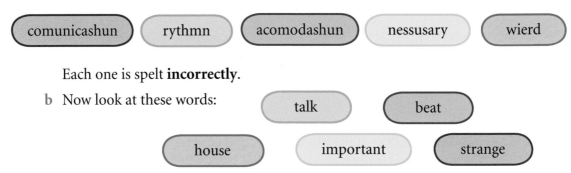

comunicashun   rythmn   acomodashun   nessusary   wierd

Each one is spelt **incorrectly**.

b Now look at these words:

talk   beat   house   important   strange

Each one is a synonym for the words above – and they are easier to spell.

c Pair each incorrectly spelt word with its matching synonym – then use a thesaurus to find its correct spelling.

Choose the best vocabulary using a thesaurus.

ACTIVITY 3

1 Sometimes a thesaurus will give you a word which you do not know. Beware of using it! Synonyms do not always have identical meanings; sometimes they have only **similar** meanings, so you can end up using a word in the wrong way.

a Look at the synonyms for the word 'huge' in the thesaurus extract on page 159.

Which words would you choose to use in these sentences?

- Her hair was so _____ it seemed to scrape the ceiling.
- Her handbag was so _____ it looked like a bin bag with handles.
- Her plate contained such a _____ quantity of food, she staggered as she carried it.

b Which words did you decide to avoid because you were unsure of their precise meaning? Look them up in a dictionary. Write a definition for each one, using **your own words**.

2 The sentences below use a lot of repetition. Using a thesaurus to select a range of vocabulary, re-write them, removing the repetition.

- She ran up to her room, screaming and screaming and screaming.
- At first he walked quickly. Later, he walked more slowly. Finally, he walked very slowly.
- It was the most horrible thing she had ever seen. It was so horrible she could not describe how horrible it was.

Use a dictionary and thesaurus to improve your vocabulary choice.

ACTIVITY 4

1 a Write seven to ten sentences describing a burglar breaking into a house.
   b Choose **five** words in your description which you think could be improved.
   c For each of the words you have chosen, use a thesaurus to find **five** appropriate synonyms.
   d Choose your favourite synonym for each word.
   e Use a dictionary to check that you are using each new word correctly.

IMPROVING YOUR LEVEL

Level 3	Level 4	Level 5	Level 6
Can use a dictionary to support understanding and spelling	Can use a dictionary and thesaurus to support understanding, spelling, and selecting vocabulary	Sometimes uses a thesaurus to select appropriate vocabulary; sometimes chooses vocabulary imprecisely	Always aims to select effective vocabulary from a broad range, sometimes using a thesaurus, occasionally imprecisely

REMEMBER

- You can use a dictionary and a thesaurus to help you with spelling.
- You can use a thesaurus to improve your choice of vocabulary.
- Beware of selecting a word from the thesaurus when you are not absolutely sure of its meaning.

AF7 Sample Answers:
Levels 3–6

The question

1 Identify the key words in the question:

Describe a school on Christmas Day
Schools are busy places during term-time. What do you think your school is like on Christmas day? You could write about:

- the playground
- the corridors
- the classrooms
- the canteen.

You will be assessed on:

- the structure of your writing
- your choice of vocabulary
- your spelling and punctuation.

2 Identify the Assessment Focus which the question is assessing.

Writing Assessment Focus 7:

Select appropriate and effective vocabulary by:
- selecting language for its effect on the reader
- selecting language appropriate to purpose and audience
- accurately using a wide vocabulary.

Level 3

- I try to choose words which will help me explain my ideas but I sometimes find it difficult to think of them.
- Sometimes I choose words because of the effect they will have on the reader.

> The school is empty. No one is there. The students and the teachers and the cleaners and the dinner ladies are all at home. There is some litter on the floor in the <u>quiet</u> classrooms. There are <u>muddy</u> footprints in the <u>quiet</u> corridors but no one is walking along them. Outside it is raining. The rain pours on the <u>quiet</u> playground. The sky is <u>dark and cloudy</u>. No cars go by because it is Christmas and everyone is at home opening their presents. It is <u>quiet</u> in the canteen. You can smell the old school dinners and the cleaning stuff they use in there.

Very little descriptive language.

Repetition could be improved with a wider choice of vocabulary.

Some language chosen for effect, mainly visual description.

Level 4

- I sometimes choose words which I think will be effective.
- I sometimes spend time thinking about or looking for the best word to suit the meaning or purpose I want to achieve.

> <u>The classrooms are</u> <u>empty</u>. <u>There is no one there. The chairs are all up on the desks and the cleaners have been.</u> The floor has been swept and mopped and you can smell the stink of disinfectant.
> The corridors are <u>empty</u>. The displays on the walls are <u>torn and hanging off</u> and look <u>messy</u>. There are no <u>running feet or ringing bells or shouting or laughing</u>. It's so silent in here you can hear the sound of a car driving past outside.
> In the <u>empty</u> playground rubbish blows around in the wind.

Some opportunities for using a range of descriptive vocabulary have been missed.

Some vocabulary chosen for effect.

Some vocabulary could be more carefully chosen.

Repetition could be improved with a wider choice of vocabulary.

Level 5

- I always choose words which I think will be effective.
- I try to use a wide range of vocabulary in my writing. Sometimes I use words when I am not entirely sure of their precise meaning.

In the classrooms, torn Christmas decorations <u>dangle</u> from the ceilings to the floor, <u>draped</u> over <u>desks</u> and chairs.
In the corridors, it's as silent <u>as a church.</u> <u>There is dust on the floor.</u>
<u>In the kitchens, you can still smell the greasy roast potatoes and lumpy gravy from the school Christmas dinner, dripped on the worktops and clogging the plug holes.</u>

> Good use of alliteration.

> Simile used but could be more original.

> <u>Wide range of vocabulary demonstrated, chosen</u> for effect.

> More descriptive vocabulary could be used.

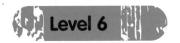
Level 6

- I always choose words which I think will be effective for the purpose and audience of my writing.
- I try to use the full breadth of my vocabulary although sometimes I use the wrong word because I am not sure of its precise meaning.

<u>The corridor is a cave,</u> footsteps <u>repealing</u> through the darkness. The squeaking wheels of a trolley <u>approach,</u> <u>whining and complaining.</u>
With a Santa hat <u>perched</u> on his round, bald head, the caretaker <u>grunts</u> and <u>groans,</u> <u>sweats</u> and <u>staggers,</u> <u>like a grumpy Father Christmas pulling his sleigh.</u> But on this trolley, <u>there are no presents neatly wrapped in patterned paper, no bulging sacks of toys, just bins overflowing with rubbish with a litter-picking stick poking out of the top.</u>

> Effective use of metaphor...

> Incorrect word choice – wrong meaning.

> ...and alliteration

> <u>Wide vocabulary used.</u>

> Effective use of personification...

> ...and simile

8.1 Spelling strategies

What am I learning?

You are learning to develop and use strategies to improve the accuracy of your spelling.

Spelling is easier for some people than others; but there are strategies you can use to help you learn spellings.

Look at some difficult spellings.

 ACTIVITY 1

1 Look at the list of words below. Which ones would you find it difficult to spell correctly? Ask a partner to test you, to help you identify them.

1 accept	9 decision	17 friend	25 receive
2 achieve	10 definite	18 grateful	26 recommend
3 appear	11 desperate	19 immediate	27 rhythm
4 address	12 disappear	20 knowledge	28 separate
5 argument	13 embarrass	21 language	29 tomatoes
6 beautiful	14 except	22 necessary	30 tomorrow
7 believe	15 fascinate	23 opportunity	
8 ceiling	16 foreign	24 permanent	

2 Look again at **five** of the words you found difficult to spell. Which **part** of the word did you get wrong?

Develop your understanding of word families.

> **prefix:** a group of letters which can be attached to the *front* of a word to change its meaning
>
> **suffix:** a group of letters which can be attached to the *end* of a word to change its meaning

1 There are thousands of words in the English language; but many of them are related to each other in *word families*. Look at these words:

believe   disbelieve   believing   unbelievable   believable   believed

Can you see the family resemblance?

a The different members of a word family have the same parent or root word: they are formed by adding **prefixes** or **suffixes**. Make a list of prefixes that can be added to the root word 'belief'.

b Now make a list of suffixes that can be added to the root word 'belief'.

c By adding prefixes or suffixes from the table on the right, how many family members can you think of which belong to these root words?

appear   embarrass   accept

Prefixes	Suffixes
dis–	-ed
un–	-ance
re–	-ment
	-able
	-ing

hope + ing = hop | ing   e

The *suffix* makes the 'o' a *long vowel sound* so the 'e' is no longer needed.

Some words double their last letter when you add *-ing*. For example, (hopping.) This is because the 'o' in hop is a *short vowel sound*.

What happens when you add *-ing* to these root words? Think about whether the new word has a long or a short vowel sound.

begin   bite   hide   step   run   pat

Choose a strategy to help you learn spellings.

Although thinking about word families can help you spell more accurately, you will need to learn new spellings. One of the best ways to learn them is:

Look → **Say** → **Cover** → **Write** → **Check**
at the word   say each letter aloud   the word up   write the word out   your spelling

1 Choose five of the words you identified in Activity 1. Use look-say-cover-write-check to learn them. Remember to concentrate on the **part** of the word that you find difficult.

There are lots of other tricks and techniques you can use to help you. The best one for you can depend on how you learn most effectively.

Visual learners learn best by looking.

The important part of look-say-cover-write-check for you is the first part: **look**. You can often tell if a word is correctly spelled if it looks right.

A good trick for you is to look for words within words. For example:

> Sep**arat**e has **a rat** in it
> bel**ie**ve has **lie** in it

Draw a word picture to help you see the word.

Auditory learners learn best by hearing.

The important part of look-say-cover-write-check for you is the second part: **say**. You can sometimes hear the letters in the right order in your head.

A good trick for you is to break a word up into syllables and pronounce them as they are spelt. For example:

> Wed-nes-day

> Op-port-u-nit-y

Kinaesthetic learners learn best by doing.

The important part of look-say-cover-write-check for you is the fourth part: **write**. You may find it easier to learn spellings if you add an extra stage: look-say-copy-cover-write-check. Copying the word out two or three times helps you get a feel for the spelling.

A good trick for you is to write out each word you need to learn on a separate piece of paper, then sort them into groups. For example, what links these words?

> immediate   fascinate   separate

Verbal learners learn best by reading and talking.

The important parts of look-say-cover-write-check for you are **look** and **say**. You need to hear the letters in the correct order to help you learn the correct spelling.

A good trick is to use a mnemonic to help you remember a spelling: a phrase or sentence which represents the different letters. For example:

Rhythm **h**elps **y**our **t**wo **h**ips **m**ove

or

Nece**ss**ary is like a shirt – **one c**ollar, **two** sleeves.

A drawing can also help you remember the mnemonic.

2 Try using each of the tips and techniques above to learn **five** of the difficult spellings you identified in Activity 1. Try to work out which learning styles suit you.

Explain the writer's choice of language

1 a Look again at the five spellings you learned in Activity 3. How many family members can you create for each one by using prefixes and suffixes?
   b Write a sentence to show the meaning of each word you created in question 1a, using a dictionary to check you are spelling them correctly.

IMPROVING YOUR LEVEL

Level 3	Level 4	Level 5	Level 6
Rarely uses spelling strategies; tends to guess phonetically	Sometimes uses spelling strategies; occasionally guesses phonetically	Is aware of appropriate spelling strategies and uses them where necessary	Is aware of areas of difficulty (eg particular spelling patterns) and uses appropriate strategies to tackle them

REMEMBER

- Identify words you find it hard to spell – and focus on the part of the word you get wrong.
- Words are often part of a family – but the spelling of the parent or root word can change.
- There are lots of different techniques you can use to learn spellings. Some will suit you better than others.

8.2 Spelling patterns

What am I learning?

You are learning to identify and use spelling patterns to help you spell more accurately.

One of the reasons spelling is so difficult in English is that, although there are rules, it can be difficult to see them.

Look at some of the problems of spelling in English.

Pronunciation – how you pronounce words can be confusing when you try to spell the words. For example:

This word: **cough**   is pronounced   (**coff**)

So you might expect this word: **tough**   to be pronounced   (**toff**)   but it isn't – it's pronounced   (**tuff**)

...which might make you think that this word: **bough**   should be pronounced   (**buff**)   but it isn't – it's pronounced   (**bow**)

1 a How many words can you think of that include the letter pattern *ear*?

   b How many different ways can *ear* be pronounced?

Develop your awareness of spelling patterns.

These are some of the most common spelling patterns in English.

Pattern	Example
ck	pick
oo	book
ea	heat
ou	mouse
ay	play
ear	bear
our	colour
ei	neighbour
au	pause
tion	reaction
able	reliable
tch	switch
ful	useful
ice	advice
cian	musician
ad	admire
ph	telephone
ious	serious

Pattern	Example
ly	slowly
oi	join
ee	seek
es	touches
ai	pain
wh	when
ow	owl
ie	chief
gh	light
sion	decision
ible	sensible
le	middle
ex	expert
ise	advise
ice	mice
al	although
ace	surface
ive	explosive

Look at each of the examples in the table above. Can you think of another word which uses the same spelling pattern but pronounces it differently? Copy and complete the table below with **five more** examples:

In the word	the spelling pattern	is pronounced	but in the word	it is pronounced
slowly	ly	lee	lying	lie

Choose a spelling pattern to work on.

1   Look again at the spelling patterns on page 170.

   • The ones in green are easier – there are lots of words which use that pattern.
   • The ones in yellow are more difficult – there are fewer words which use that pattern.
   • The ones in pink are the hardest – there are even fewer words which use that pattern.

   a   Choose a spelling pattern which you find challenging. How many words can you think of which contain that spelling pattern?

   • For green spelling patterns, aim for **15** words.
   • For yellow spelling patterns, aim for **10** words.
   • For pink spelling patterns, aim for **5** words.

   Write each one on a small slip of paper.

   b   Sort all your words into pronunciation groups. For example:

   heat and *cream* belong in the same group because the *ea* pattern is pronounced *ee* in both words. However, *head* should be placed in a different group because the *ea* pattern is pronounced *e*.

   c   Look at each of your pronunciation groups. Can you think of any other words which have a similar pronunciation but use a different spelling? For example:

   the *-ay* sound can be spelt: -ay-   -ai-   -ei-

   as in the word: play   pain   eight

   d   Put all your spellings back in one group. Can you spot any other patterns?

   • Do the meanings of the words have anything in common? For example, words ending in *-cian* are often to do with people's jobs: magician, musician, etc.
   • Does the spelling pattern usually come at the start, the middle or the end of the word? For example, *-ly* usually comes at the end of a word: lovely, ugly, etc.
   • Are most of the words of the same type: all nouns, verbs, adverbs or adjectives? For example, words ending in *-ious* are usually adjectives: serious, delicious.

Use spelling patterns in your writing.

1 a Look again at the list of spellings which you collected in your answer to Activity 3, question 1a. Write a sentence using as many of them as you can.
   b Now, repeat the process, using a different spelling pattern.

IMPROVING YOUR LEVEL

Level 3	Level 4	Level 5	Level 6
Is aware of a limited range of high frequency spelling patterns	Is aware of a range of high frequency spelling patterns	Is aware of a range of mid and high frequency spelling patterns, including inflections	Is aware of the majority of mid and high frequency spelling patterns, including inflections

REMEMBER

- Learning spelling patterns and the words that use them can improve your spelling.
- Pronunciation is not always a good guide for spelling patterns.
- Always use a teacher or partner to check any spelling you are not sure about.

AF8 Sample Answers: Levels 3–6

The text

A national newspaper is running a competition, inviting teenagers to write an article for publication. This is what appeared in the newspaper:

Teenage writers – see your work in print

Today we launch a competition, inviting teenage writers to write a short article (200–300 words) to be published in our Saturday edition later in the year.

We would like you to explain who your hero is and why.

Who do you admire? Who is your role model? Whose skills or talents do you think deserve hero status?

Write and let us know and you could see your work in print in just a couple of months.

The question

1 Identify the key words in the question: audience, purpose and form.

Write the article, explaining who your hero is and why.

2 Identify the Assessment Focus which the question is assessing.

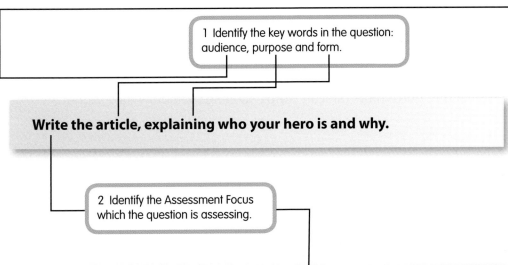

Writing Assessment Focus 6:

Writing Assessment Focus 1:
* Spelling based on knowledge of spelling patterns.
* Knowledge of more unusual and irregular spellings.

Level 3

- I can usually spell some of the words which I often see, for example, you, because, although.
- I sometimes find it difficult to spell words where the endings have changed, for example, plurals (*-es*, *-ies*), change of tense (*-ied*, *-ing*)
- I usually guess more difficult words, spelling them how they sound.

> My hero is Michael Owen. He is great <u>becuase</u> he is <u>won</u> of the best footballers around. He plays for Newcastle United and England and he is won of the top goal scorers for England. When I leave school I <u>woud</u> like to be a <u>profeshonal</u> footballer becuase I have <u>playd</u> for the school and I have <u>tryed</u> realy hard.

High frequency word incorrectly spelt.

Incorrect homophone chosen.

Incorrect spelling of verb endings in past tense.

More difficult word spelt phonetically.

Level 4

- I can usually spell:
  - words which I often see, for example, you, because, although
  - most adverbs which end in *-ly*.
- I sometimes find it difficult to spell:
  - words which sound the same as other words (homophones), for example, they're/their/there; to/too/two; of/have/off
  - words where the endings have changed, for example, plurals (*-es*, *-ies*), change of tense (*–ied*, *–ing*).
- I sometimes guess more difficult words, spelling them how they sound.

> My hero is my mum. She works <u>really</u> hard all day and then she has to collect my <u>little</u> brother from my auntys house and come home and put up with us <u>argueing</u> and <u>fighting</u>. <u>There</u> are <u>two</u> other reasons I love and admire my mum – her cooking and her putting up with my dad. <u>Their</u> always joking and shouting and messing around. <u>Somtimes</u> she falls asleep after tea because she is <u>to</u> tired after her busy day. 'I'm <u>exorsted</u>' she says. Then she starts snoring.

Some spelling patterns used accurately.

Does not drop th 'e' when adding suffix.

More difficult word spelt phonetically.

Compound word incorrectly spelt: some + times.

Some homophones correctly spelt – some not.

Level 5

- I can always spell:
  - words which I often see, for example, you, because, although
  - words where the endings have changed, for example, plurals (-es, -ies), change of tense (-ied, -ing)
  - most words with suffixes, for example, -able/-ible; -ion/-ian
  - most words with prefixes, for example, dis-, un-, ex-.
- I sometimes find it difficult to spell:
  - words with prefixes which make double consonants, for example, irregular, unnecessary.
- Occasionally I guess more difficult words, spelling them how they sound.

> My hero is James Bond. I know he is only a <u>fictional</u> character but I would still like to be like him. He's strong and <u>adventurous.</u> I wouldn't want to be tied up and tortured, which seems to happen in most of his films, but the rest of his life is full of <u>explosive excitment.</u> He does do some bad things but he does them for the right reasons. He is a man with a <u>conshience.</u> I would also like to have his <u>incredible</u> gadgets and drive his car. I would love to have an <u>ejecter</u> seat, a radar and some missiles in my car. He also meets lots of beautiful women.

More difficult word using correct spelling patterns.

Incorrect use of spelling pattern.

More difficult word spelt phonetically.

Level 6

- I usually spell most words correctly.
- Occasionally I spell more difficult or unusual words incorrectly.

> My hero, although I hate to admit it and would never tell him, is my brother. He got brilliant GCSE results, and will <u>probably</u> get brilliant A Level results. But he isn't a hermit, <u>permanently</u> sitting alone at his desk. He plays rugby and football for the school. He's got loads of good friends who he goes out with, and <u>they're</u> always laughing. He is <u>sucessful</u> and happy – the perfect <u>combination.</u>

Accurate use of patterns in more challenging spellings.

Only one error – an unusual spelling.

Correct choice of homophone.

Writing skills practice
Imagine, entertain and explore

These are the key features and skills of successful writing and, in particular, of writing to imagine, entertain and explore. You can find activities to develop these skills here.

Assessment focus	Key feature	Relevant pages	Learn how:
1 Imagine	Plan	1.1 pages 6–9	to plan and sequence your ideas
	Story structure	1.2 pages 10–14	narrative fiction can be structured
		1.3 pages 15–18	to manipulate narrative fiction structure to change the reader's response to your story
	Character	1.4 pages 19–22	writers create characters, narrators and their relationship with the reader
		1.5 pages 23–26	to use a range of techniques for building an effective character
	Setting and atmosphere	1.6 pages 27–30	writers select details to create an effective setting in a story
2 Purpose, audience and form	Answer the question	2.1 pages 34–38	to read a writing task and identify the purpose, audience and form required
	Be aware of key features and appropriate register	2.2 pages 39–42	to structure and shape your writing for specific purposes and audiences
	Select appropriate material	2.3 pages 43–47	to select from a range of points depending on your audience
4 Paragraphs	Paragraph	4.1 pages 88–91	to organise your writing in paragraphs to support meaning and for effect
	Connect sentences within paragraphs	4.3 pages 96–98	to use pronouns and synonyms to give your paragraphs cohesion
5 Sentences	Use a range of sentence types and lengths	5.1 pages 102–105	to vary sentence length and structure for effect
		5.2 pages 106–109	to use a range of sentence types for variety and effect
	Rhetorical devices	5.3 pages 110–113	to use a range of rhetorical devices at sentence level
	Select an appropriate register, usually standard English	5.4 pages 114–117	to adapt the register of your writing depending on your audience
6 Punctuation	Punctuate correctly	6.1–6.5 pages 122–141	to use a range of punctuation accurately

Assessment focus	Key feature	Relevant pages	Learn how:
7 Vocabulary	Choose your vocabulary	7.1 pages 145–148	to select the best words in your writing, thinking about their effect.
	Rhetorical devices	7.2 pages 149–152	to use a range of rhetorical devices at word level
	Use simile, metaphor or personification	7.3 pages 153–157	to use figurative language to create a strong image in your reader's mind
	Check your work and develop vocabulary	7.4 pages 158–161	to use a dictionary and thesaurus to improve the accuracy and breadth of your vocabulary choice
8 Spelling	Spell accurately	8.1–8.2 pages 165–172	to improve and develop spelling strategies

QUESTIONS

Before you attempt any of the tasks that follow, think about the **genre** of the story you are going to write. Some tasks may tell you the genre of story you need to write; in other tasks you may be able to choose from several different genres (see the list below). Remember to choose characters, settings and events appropriate to the genre.

genre: the type of film or story

adventure   fairy tale   romance   horror

fantasy   science fiction   mystery   crime   ghost

Tip!

It's a good idea to come up with two or even three ideas for your story before you put in the hard work on planning it: first ideas aren't always the best ideas! That way, you are less likely to plan or even write a story that you don't really like.

1   Your teacher has received an email from a major publisher:

We are planning a new collection of short stories to be published next year. The collection will be called *Shadows* and will contain around 30 short stories, all entitled *The Shadow*. The stories will be written by and for secondary school students aged 12–14. We would like your students to contribute short stories to be considered for publication.

Write a short story of around 300 to 500 words entitled *The Shadow*. Remember:

• your story should appeal to 12 to 14-year-olds.
• your story should be imaginative and entertaining
• your story should be between 300 and 500 words.

2   Look at this student's idea for a short story.

> Wake up one morning, open curtains, see most amazing sight outside bedroom window…

Use this idea to plan and write your own short story.
Think about these questions to help you.

• What do you see outside your window?
• What problems or consequences are created by what you see?
• What do you decide to do about it?

Aim to make your story imaginative and entertaining, and between 400 and 800 words long.

3   Write a story which begins with the line:

> Something woke me up. It was a voice I did not recognise.

Before you begin writing, consider the following questions to help you plan your story.

• Where are you when you are woken? At home in bed, or somewhere else?
• Whose voice is it that you hear? Your decision will affect the genre of your story: will it be a ghost story, an adventure story, or a different genre?

4 Look at these newspaper headlines:

The Most Expensive Take Away in the World

UFO Picture is a Hoax, Say Experts

'I'LL PAY IT ALL BACK'

HELP! SOMEONE'S STOLEN MY IDENTITY!

Write a story which could begin or end with the appearance of one of these headlines in a newspaper.

5 Look at this collection of objects:

- a jewel
- a bottle of ketchup
- a bunch of flowers
- a birthday cake
- a pair of gloves
- a book
- a key
- a guitar
- a cat
- a wad of money
- a spade

Choose as many or as few of these objects as you like and write a story about them.

6 Look at the paintings below. Answer the questions after each one to help you imagine a story behind the painting.

- Where might this man be? Think about what is around him that is not shown in the picture.
- Who is this man? What is he doing? Looking for something? Waiting for someone?
- How do you think the man is feeling? What might have made him feel that way?
- Does this picture show the begining of his story? Or the end?

The Wanderer Above the Sea of Fog by Caspar David Friedrich

Rough Sea at Etreat by Claude Monet

- How would you describe the weather in this image?
- Who is this crowd of people? Why are they there?
- Has something happened? Or are they expecting something to happen?

Write a story based on one of these paintings.

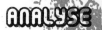

Analyse

These are the key features and skills of successful writing and, in particular, of writing to analyse. You can find activities to develop these skills here.

Assessment focus	Key feature	Relevant pages	Learn how to:
1 Imagine	Plan	1.1 pages 6–9	plan and sequence your ideas
2 Purpose, audience and form	Answer the question	2.1 pages 34–38	read a writing task and identify the purpose, audience and form required
	Be aware of key features and appropriate register	2.2 pages 39–42	structure and shape your writing for specific purposes and audiences
	Select appropriate material	2.3 pages 43–47	select from a range of points depending on your audience
	Present your opinion using modals, imperatives and the first person	2.4 pages 48–52	give your opinion in a range of ways
3 Structure	Introduce and conclude your writing	3.1 pages 68–72	organise the structure of your writing
	Use connectives and linking phrases	3.3 pages 77–80	develop your use and range of connectives
		3.4 pages 81–84	use a variety of different methods to link your ideas and give your writing cohesion
4 Paragraphs	Paragraph	4.1 pages 88–91	organise your writing in paragraphs to support meaning and for effect
	Use point-evidence-explain paragraphs	4.2 pages 92–95	organise your points and ideas in effective paragraphs
	Connect sentences within paragraphs	4.3 pages 96–98	use pronouns and synonyms to give your paragraphs cohesion
5 Sentences	Use a range of sentence types and lengths	5.1 pages 102–105	vary sentence length and structure for effect
		5.2 pages 106–109	use a range of sentence types for variety and effect
	Select an appropriate register, usually standard English	5.4 pages 114–117	adapt the register of your writing depending on your audience
6 Punctuation	Punctuate correctly	6.1–6.5 pages 122–141	use a range of punctuation accurately
7 Vocabulary	Choose your vocabulary	7.1 pages 145–148	select the best words in your writing, thinking about their effect
	Check your work and develop vocabulary	7.4 pages 158–161	use a dictionary and thesaurus to improve the accuracy and breadth of your vocabulary choice
8 Spelling	Spell accurately	8.1–8.2 pages 165–172	improve and develop spelling strategies

QUESTIONS

A class of secondary school students were asked what they thought about reading. These are some of the things they wrote:

- Reading is boring.

- I haven't got time to read.

- I used to like reading but I can't find anything I like now I'm a bit older.

- I prefer watching telly or playing on my games console.

- Everyone likes a good story.

- If you look hard enough, there are loads of good books to choose from. I like biographies.

- I find reading really hard. The books I can read are for younger kids and the books I want to read are too difficult.

- Sometimes it's difficult to get into a book. But if you find one you really like, they're much better than films or computer games. They can take you to another world.

What do you think? Write a report *analysing* why teenagers do not read as much as younger children or adults – and what can be done to encourage them to read more. You could write about:

- your reading habits. Do you read for pleasure? If not, why not? If you do, what is it you like about reading?
- your opinion on the kinds of books that are currently available for teenagers. You could write about a book you have enjoyed and a book you did not like.
- the kinds of books teenagers like. What kinds of books should writers be writing for teenagers?
- what parents, teachers and publishers should do to encourage teenagers to read more.

2 Read these two extracts from letters which were recently published in a national newspaper.

> Our schools cost a fortune to run and maintain. Surely now that so much learning is done online in other situations, it is time to close our state schools and educate our children via the internet. Students could attend virtual lessons, submit homework online and learn at their own pace. There would be an end to poor behaviour, bullying and

> I read the letter you published yesterday with interest. The writer is, however, assuming that schools exist simply to teach our children how to read, write and add up. Schools do far more than this which would all be lost if children were educated electronically at home. Schools teach our children to work together, to learn together, to play together. Socialising with other children and adults is vital for children to

Write a report analysing the pros and cons of closing schools and replacing them with virtual schools, teaching students using the Internet.
You could write about:

- the advantages of learning via the Internet
- the advantages of learning at school
- which, in your opinion, is the best option.

Review

These are the key features and skills of successful writing and, in particular, of writing to review. You can find activities to develop these skills here.

Assessment focus	Key feature	Relevant pages	Learn how to:
1 Imagine	Plan	1.1 pages 6–9	plan and sequence your ideas
2 Purpose, audience and form	Answer the question	2.1 pages 34–38	read a writing task and identify the purpose, audience and form required
	Be aware of key features and appropriate register	2.2 pages 39–42	structure and shape your writing for specific purposes and audiences
	Select appropriate material	2.3 pages 43–47	select from a range of points depending on your audience
	Present your opinion using modals, imperatives and the first person	2.4 pages 48–52	give your opinion in a range of ways
3 Structure	Introduce and conclude your writing	3.1 pages 68–72	organise the structure of your writing
	Use connectives and linking phrases	3.3 pages 77–80	develop your use and range of connectives
		3.4 pages 81–84	use a variety of different methods to link your ideas and give your writing cohesion
4 Paragraphs	Paragraph	4.1 pages 88–91	organise your writing in paragraphs to support meaning and for effect
	Use point-evidence-explain paragraphs	4.2 pages 92–95	organise your points and ideas in effective paragraphs
	Connect sentences within paragraphs	4.3 pages 96–98	use pronouns and synonyms to give your paragraphs cohesion
5 Sentences	Use a range of sentence types and lengths	5.1 pages 102–105	vary sentence length and structure for effect
		5.2 pages 106–109	use a range of sentence types for variety and effect
	Rhetorical devices	5.3 pages 110–113	use a range of rhetorical devices at sentence level
	Select an appropriate register, usually standard English	5.4 pages 114–117	adapt the register of your writing depending on your audience

Assessment focus	Key feature	Relevant pages	Learn how to:
6 Punctuation	Punctuate correctly	6.1–6.5 pages 122–141	use a range of punctuation accurately
7 Vocabulary	Choose your vocabulary	7.1 pages 145–148	select the best words in your writing, thinking about their effect
	Rhetorical devices	7.2 pages 149–152	use a range of rhetorical devices in your writing
	Check your work and develop vocabulary	7.4 pages 158–161	use a dictionary and thesaurus to improve the accuracy and breadth of your vocabulary choice
8 Spelling	Spell accurately	8.1–8.2 pages 165–172	improve and develop spelling strategies

QUESTIONS

My Perfect Party

Give yourself a party to remember!

Whatever your age, from 1 to 101, whatever the occasion, from birthdays to weddings, we can organise you an unforgettable party. Where do you want to go? What do you want to do? What do you want to eat, drink, listen and dance to? Tell us what you want – and then leave the rest to us. Prices to suit all pockets.

Win! Win! Win! Tell us about your perfect party in 100 words or less and you could win the party of your dreams. Our judges will choose the best entry – and the winner will get the party they asked for*, absolutely free!
*terms and conditions apply

a Write a description of your perfect party to enter into the 'My Perfect Party' competition.

b Congratulations, you won! Your party has taken place and My Perfect Party have asked you to write a review of it which they can use in their next advertising campaign.

Write a positive or negative review of your party.
Aim to write about 300 to 500 words. Think about these questions to help you plan your review:

- Did they organise everything you asked for?
- Was it just how you imagined it would be?
- Were the venue, food and entertainment of the quality you expected?
- Did you and your guests enjoy themselves?
- Would you ask My Perfect Party to organise another celebration for you?

eating out in
bRITAIN

A guide to Britains best Resturant, Pub and Cafe food.

The publishers of Eating Out in Britain need your help.

Had a brilliant burger? A perfect pizza? Or a chewy Chinese? Fabulous fish and chips? Or a crummy curry?

Write a 300 to 500-word review of a meal you have loved or loathed and you could see your opinions in print!

Write a positive or negative review to send to the publishers of *Eating Out in Britain*.
It could be a meal you have eaten in a restaurant or a takeaway you have eaten at home. You could write about:

- the choice of food available
- the quality of the food
- the service you received from the restaurant staff (were they friendly, helpful and efficient?)
- the cleanliness and comfort of the restaurant in which you ate or bought your meal
- whether you would recommend this restaurant.

Inform

These are the key features and skills of successful writing and, in particular, of writing to inform. You can find activities to develop these skills here.

Assessment focus	Key feature	Relevant pages	Learn how to:
1 Imagine	Plan	1.1 pages 6–9	plan and sequence your ideas
2 Purpose, audience and form	Answer the question	2.1 pages 34–38	read a writing task and identify the purpose, audience and form required
	Be aware of key features and appropriate register	2.2 pages 39–42	structure and shape your writing for specific purposes and audiences
	Select appropriate material	2.3 pages 43–47	select from a range of points depending on your audience
3 Structure	Introduce and conclude your writing	2.4 pages 48–52	organise the structure of your writing
	Present your writing effectively	3.1 pages 68–72	adapt layout and presentation to your purpose and audience
	Use connectives and linking phrases	3.3 pages 77–80	develop your use and range of connectives
		3.4 pages 81–84	use a variety of different methods to link your ideas and give your writing cohesion
4 Paragraphs	Paragraph	4.1 pages 88–91	organise your writing in paragraphs to support meaning and for effect
	Use topic-sentence-expand paragraphs	4.2 pages 92–95	organise your points and ideas in effective paragraphs
	Connect sentences within paragraphs	4.3 pages 96–98	use pronouns and synonyms to give your paragraphs cohesion
5 Sentences	Use a range of sentence types and lengths	5.1 pages 102–105	vary sentence length and structure for effect
		5.2 pages 106–109	use a range of sentence types for variety and effect
	Select an appropriate register, usually standard English	5.4 pages 114–117	adapt the register of your writing depending on your audience
6 Punctuation	Punctuate correctly	6.1–6.5 pages 122–141	use a range of punctuation accurately
7 Vocabulary	Choose your vocabulary	7.1 pages 145–148	select the best words in your writing, thinking about their effect
	Check your work and develop vocabulary	7.4 pages 158–161	use a dictionary and thesaurus to improve the accuracy and breadth of your vocabulary choice
8 Spelling	Spell accurately	8.1–8.2 pages 165–172	improve and develop spelling strategies

QUESTIONS

When Year 7 students arrive at secondary schools in September for the first time, they are usually given an information leaflet telling them all about their new school. It often tells them things such as:

- what subjects they will be learning
- how much homework they will be given
- what equipment they will need.

But is that the most important information for new students? What do those new Year 7s *really* need to know to survive and make the most of their time at your school?

Write an information guide for them, sharing everything you have learned since you arrived at your school. In it you could tell them:

- Where should they go? What should they do? How should they behave?
- How can they avoid getting into trouble?
- Where are the best places to hang around at break and lunch?
- What should they do if they get a detention?
- Anything else which you think is important or interesting.

School is a place where teachers teach students what they need to know. But students know a lot too. What are you an expert on?

Your school has decided to ask students to share their knowledge with each other by producing a series of information leaflets featuring all the essential information they will need. The leaflets will be kept in the school library to be read and used by other students.

Write the text for a leaflet to inform other students at your school about the topic of your choice.
You could produce a leaflet about:

- a sport, hobby or interest which you know a lot about
- the best new gadgets
- how to get the most out of your computer
- the life of a well-known sports person or musician
- anything that you know about…

You could include illustrations or diagrams to give your reader even more information.

Explain

These are the key features and skills of successful writing and, in particular, of writing to explain. You can find activities to develop these skills here.

Assessment focus	Key feature	Relevant pages	Learn how to:
1 Imagine	Plan	1.1 pages 6–9	plan and sequence your ideas
2 Purpose, audience and form	Answer the question	2.1 pages 34–38	read a writing task and identify the purpose, audience and form required
	Be aware of key features and appropriate register	2.2 pages 39–42	structure and shape your writing for specific purposes and audiences
	Select appropriate material	2.3 pages 43–47	select from a range of points depending on your audience
3 Structure	Introduce and conclude your writing	3.1 pages 68–72	organise the structure of your writing
	Use connectives and linking phrases	3.3 pages 77–80	develop your use and range of connectives
		3.4 pages 81–84	use a variety of different methods to link your ideas and give your writing cohesion
4 Paragraphs	Paragraph	4.1 pages 88–91	organise your writing in paragraphs to support meaning and for effect
	Use topic-sentence-expand paragraphs	4.2 pages 92–95	organise your points and ideas in effective paragraphs
	Connect sentences within paragraphs	4.3 pages 96–98	use pronouns and synonyms to give your paragraphs cohesion
5 Sentences	Use a range of sentence types and lengths	5.1 pages 102–105	vary sentence length and structure for effect
		5.2 pages 106–109	use a range of sentence types for variety and effect
	Select an appropriate register, usually standard English	5.4 pages 114–117	adapt the register of your writing depending on your audience
6 Punctuation	Punctuate correctly	6.1–6.5 pages 122–141	use a range of punctuation accurately
7 Vocabulary	Choose your vocabulary	7.1 pages 145–148	select the best words in your writing, thinking about their effect
	Check your work and develop vocabulary	7.4 pages 158–161	use a dictionary and thesaurus to improve the accuracy and breadth of your vocabulary choice
8 Spelling	Spell accurately	8.1–8.2 pages 165–172	improve and develop spelling strategies

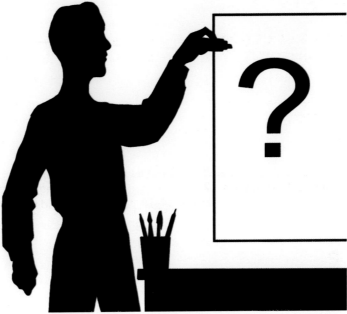

The *Teacher's Times* Wants Your Students' Views

We all think we know what makes a good teacher. But what do your students think? This week, we're running a competition in which we're inviting all secondary school students to write an article of 300 to 500 words, explaining what they think makes a great teacher. The best entries will be published over the next few weeks.

Write your article explaining what you think makes a good teacher.

You could write about:

- how a good teacher interacts with their students
- the different kinds of activities and tasks which good teachers set in their lessons
- how a good teacher ensures that students behave well in their lessons
- what a good teacher's classroom looks like
- the difference a good teacher can make to the lives of their students.

2 Your careers advisor has given you a letter.

INGLETON HIGH SCHOOL
INGLETON
NORTH YORKSHIRE
BD1 4PY
Head Teacher:
JANE P. DONE

13 March 2009

Dear Student

What will you do when you leave school? It's important to set yourself goals and to think about your future, especially when you are choosing the subjects you will study in Years 10 and 11 and beyond.

To help you choose and achieve your goals, I'd like you to write to me explaining:

- what you see yourself doing in ten years' time
- what you will have to achieve over the next ten years to reach this goal
- how you will achieve these things
- how the school can help you.

I look forward to hearing from you.

Yours faithfully

Write the letter to the school careers advisor, explaining what you would like your future to hold and how you intend to achieve it. Aim to write about 300 to 500 words.

Describe

These are the key features and skills of successful writing and, in particular, of writing to describe. You can find activities to develop these skills here.

Assessment focus	Key feature	Relevant pages	Learn how to:
1 Imagine	Plan	1.1 pages 6–9	plan and sequence your ideas
2 Purpose, audience and form	Answer the question	2.1 pages 34–38	read a writing task and identify the purpose, audience and form required
	Be aware of key features and appropriate register	2.2 pages 39–42	structure and shape your writing for specific purposes and audiences
	Select appropriate material	2.3 pages 43–47	select from a range of points depending on your audience
3 Structure	Introduce and conclude your writing	3.1 pages 68–72	organise the structure of your writing
	Use connectives and linking phrases	3.3 pages 77–80	develop your use and range of connectives
		3.4 pages 81–84	use a variety of different methods to link your ideas and give your writing cohesion
4 Paragraphs	Paragraph	4.1 pages 88–91	organise your writing in paragraphs to support meaning and for effect
	Use topic-sentence-expand paragraphs	4.2 pages 92–95	organise your points and ideas in effective paragraphs
	Connect sentences within paragraphs	4.3 pages 96–98	use pronouns and synonyms to give your paragraphs cohesion
5 Sentences	Use a range of sentence types and lengths	5.1 pages 102–105	vary sentence length and structure for effect
		5.2 pages 106–109	use a range of sentence types for variety and effect
	Rhetorical devices	5.3 pages 110–113	use a range of rhetorical devices at sentence level
	Select an appropriate register, usually standard English	5.4 pages 114–117	adapt the register of your writing depending on your audience
6 Punctuation	Punctuate correctly	6.1–6.5 pages 122–141	use a range of punctuation accurately

7 Vocabulary	Choose your vocabulary	7.1 pages 145–148	select the best words in your writing, thinking about their effect
	Rhetorical devices	7.2 pages 149–152	use a range of rhetorical devices at word level
	Use simile, metaphor or personification	7.3 pages 153–157	use figurative language to create a strong image in your reader's mind
	Check your work and develop vocabulary	7.4 pages 158–161	use a dictionary and thesaurus to improve the accuracy and breadth of your vocabulary choice
8 Spelling	Spell accurately	8.1–8.2 pages 165–172	improve and develop spelling strategies

QUESTIONS

The Great Plague Factsheet

Plague broke out in London in spring 1665, carried by the fleas which infested the rats which came on ships from Holland. The houses of London were tightly packed along narrow streets with no sanitation: ideal conditions for the spread of disease.

The summer of 1665 was extremely hot. The fleas bred and spread very successfully and the death toll rose rapidly. People panicked and the wealthy fled from the city in their thousands.

The front doors of houses where plague victims lived were marked with a red cross. People only went out when it was an absolute necessity. Carts drove through the streets after dark, the drivers calling 'bring out your dead', collecting the corpses of plague victims and taking them to be buried in mass graves as the graveyards were all full.

In October 1665, Samuel Pepys wrote in his diary: 'How empty the streets are... so many poor sick people in the streets, full of sores, and so many sad stories overheard as I walk, everybody talking of this dead, and that man sick, and so many in this place, and so many in that. And they tell me that in Westminster there is never a physician, and but one apothecary left, all being dead.'

Write a description of a walk through the streets of London in summer 1665. Remember: you should write a description of the scene, *not* a story.

You should write about:
* the streets in the daytime
* the streets at night-time
* the sights, sounds and smells of the city.

Aim to write about 300 to 500 words.

2 Write a description of your school canteen during a busy lunchtime.
Remember: you are writing a description, *not* a story.

You could write about:

- the weather outside (how does it affect the canteen and the students?)
- the students queuing and eating
- the teachers supervising
- the catering staff cooking and serving
- the sights, sounds and smells of the canteen.

Aim to write about 300 to 500 words.

3 Write a description of your home in the middle of the night. Think about the atmosphere you want to create. Will it be quiet and peaceful, or silent and spooky?
Remember: you are writing a description, *not* a story.

You could describe:

- outside your home
- inside your home
- people sleeping
- the sights, sounds and smells of your home.

Argue

These are the key features and skills of successful writing and, in particular, of writing to argue. You can find activities to develop these skills here.

Assessment focus	Key feature	Relevant pages	Learn how to:
1 Imagine	Plan	1.1 pages 6–9	plan and sequence your ideas
2 Purpose, audience and form	Answer the question	2.1 pages 34–38	read a writing task and identify the purpose, audience and form required
	Be aware of key features and appropriate register	2.2 pages 39–42	structure and shape your writing for specific purposes and audiences
	Select appropriate material	2.3 pages 43–47	select from a range of points depending on your audience
	Present your opinion using modals, imperatives and the first person	2.4 pages 48–52	give your opinion in a range of ways
		2.5 pages 53–56	use facts and opinions, and disguise opinions as facts
	Develop and sequence your opinion	2.6 pages 57–60	develop and express your own point of view
	Use the passive voice to strengthen your point of view	2.7 pages 61–64	use the passive voice for effect
3 Structure	Introduce and conclude your writing	3.1 pages 68–72	organise the structure of your writing
	Use connectives and linking phrases	3.3 pages 77–80	develop your use and range of connectives
		3.4 pages 81–84	use a variety of different methods to link your ideas and give your writing cohesion
4 Paragraphs	Paragraph	4.1 pages 88–91	organise your writing in paragraphs to support meaning and for effect
	Use point-evidence-explain paragraphs	4.2 pages 92–95	organise your points and ideas in effective paragraphs
	Connect sentences within paragraphs	4.3 pages 96–98	use pronouns and synonyms to give your paragraphs cohesion
5 Sentences	Use a range of sentence types and lengths	5.1 pages 102–105	vary sentence length and structure for effect
		5.2 pages 106–109	use a range of sentence types for variety and effect
	Rhetorical devices	5.3 pages 110–113	adapt the register of your writing depending on your audience
	Select an appropriate register, usually standard English	5.4 pages 114–117	adapt the register of your writing depending on your audience

6 Punctuation	Punctuate correctly	6.1–6.5 pages 122–141	use a range of punctuation accurately
7 Vocabulary	Choose your vocabulary	7.1 pages 145–148	select the best words in your writing, thinking about their effect
	Rhetorical devices	7.2 pages 149–152	use a range of rhetorical devices at word level
	Check your work and develop vocabulary	7.4 pages 158–161	use a dictionary and thesaurus to improve the accuracy and breadth of your vocabulary choice
8 Spelling	Spell accurately	8.1–8.2 pages 165–172	improve and develop spelling strategies

QUESTIONS

A letter has been given to the students at your school to take home.

BENTHAM
COMMUNITY COLLEGE

HIGH BENTHAM
LANCASHIRE, LA6 3PD
Head Teacher:
KEITH LORD

18 February 2009

Dear Students, Parents and Guardians

As you may be aware, our school budget has been cut again and we have fewer pupils joining us next year. As a result, the school faces some difficult financial choices if we are to maintain the high standard of education which our students currently enjoy.

A local property developer has shown interest in purchasing the school's playing fields with a view to building 30 houses and flats. If we were to accept this offer it would make a significant contribution to the school's finances. If we decide against the offer, we will need to look elsewhere for savings. This could involve teacher redundancies, a consequent increase in class sizes, a reduction in the choice of subjects we can offer, fewer teaching resources, particularly in ICT, and in vocational courses such as construction and horticulture.

Clearly this is not a decision the school governors will take lightly and we must weigh up the obvious benefits of the sale against the obvious disadvantages. We would like to hear your views. If you would like to express an opinion, please write to me at the above address within 30 days of the date on this letter. I look forward to hearing from you.

Write a letter to your head teacher arguing *for* or *against* the sale of the school playing fields to help solve your school's financial problems.

Your head teacher has written a letter to the parents and guardians of students at your school.

Palatine

HIGH SCHOOL

ESSEX
CM20 7HY
Head Teacher:
ELIZABETH BARLEY

10 May 2009

Dear Parents and Guardians

As I am sure you are aware, uniform is a major focus of the school this year. While we are delighted with the appearance of the majority of our students, there is still a significant problem with a minority of students wearing inappropriate footwear and outdoor coats, in particular trainers and hooded tops.

As a result, the school governors have decided to extend the range of school uniform which we require **all** students to wear. From September, students must wear shoes and outdoor coats chosen from an approved range which will be available from the school and from local stockists. Please be assured that these items have been chosen for their quality, value and appropriateness. Further details will be available later this year.

We recognise that this is an additional cost to parents. Financial support is, as always, available for parents on lower incomes by applying to the school finance office at the above address.

Yours sincerely

Write a letter to your head teacher arguing *for* or *against* the introduction of uniform shoes and overcoats.

Persuade

These are the key features and skills of successful writing and, in particular, of writing to persuade. You can find activities to develop these skills here.

Assessment focus	Key feature	Relevant pages	Learn how to:
1 Imagine	Plan	1.1 pages 6–9	plan and sequence your ideas
2 Purpose, audience and form	Answer the question	2.1 pages 34–38	read a writing task and identify the purpose, audience and form required
	Be aware of key features and appropriate register	2.2 pages 39–42	structure and shape your writing for specific purposes and audiences
	Select appropriate material	2.3 pages 43–47	select from a range of points depending on your audience
	Present your opinion using modals, imperatives and the first person	2.4 pages 48–52	give your opinion in a range of ways
		2.5 pages 53–56	use facts and opinions, and disguise opinions as facts
	Develop and sequence your opinion	2.6 pages 57–60	develop and express your own point of view
	Use the passive voice to strengthen your point of view	2.7 pages 61–64	use the passive voice for effect
3 Structure	Introduce and conclude your writing	3.1 pages 68–72	organise the structure of your writing
	Use connectives and linking phrases	3.3 pages 77–80	develop your use and range of connectives
		3.4 pages 81–84	use a variety of different methods to link your ideas and give your writing cohesion
4 Paragraphs	Paragraph	4.1 pages 88–91	organise your writing in paragraphs to support meaning and for effect
	Use point-evidence-explain paragraphs	4.2 pages 92–95	organise your points and ideas in effective paragraphs
	Connect sentences within paragraphs	4.3 pages 96–98	use pronouns and synonyms to give your paragraphs cohesion

5 Sentences	Use a range of sentence types and lengths	5.1 pages 102–105	vary sentence length and structure for effect
		5.2 pages 106–109	use a range of sentence types for variety and effect
	Rhetorical devices	5.3 pages 110–113	use a range of rhetorical devices at sentence level
	Select an appropriate register, usually standard English	5.4 pages 114–117	adapt the register of your writing depending on your audience
6 Punctuation	Punctuate correctly	6.1–6.5 pages 122–141	use a range of punctuation accurately
7 Vocabulary	Choose your vocabulary	7.1 pages 145–148	select the best words in your writing, thinking about their effect
	Rhetorical devices	7.2 pages 149–152	use a range of rhetorical devices at word level
	Check your work and develop vocabulary	7.4 pages 158–161	use a dictionary and thesaurus to improve the accuracy and breadth of your vocabulary choice
8 Spelling	Spell accurately	8.1–8.2 pages 165–172	improve and develop spelling strategies

QUESTIONS

At a recent meeting of the Student Council, it was announced that from the start of the new school year the school timetable will be reorganised, making room for one more lesson every week. Which subject do you think the extra lesson should be given to? Look at this extract from the minutes of the meeting in which the views of different members of the school council were recorded:

The following subjects were suggested:

- English, Maths or Science: the most important subjects for future employment
- ICT: a really important skill for our future lives
- History or Geography: the teachers are always complaining there is not enough time to cover the syllabus
- A new subject – suggestions included: managing your money, a practical skill like bricklaying or plumbing, key skills (spelling, revising for exams, etc.).

What do you think? Write a letter to the school council, persuading them to choose your suggestion.

2 What's the best job that you could possibly dream of doing after you have completed your education?

a Imagine you are the employer, advertising this dream job. Write a newspaper advertisement *persuading* people to apply for the position. Remember to give all the important details, including:

- what skills the applicants will need
- what the job will involve
- the annual salary and any other benefits.

b Now write a letter of application, applying for the job. To *persuade* the employer that you are the right person, you will need to explain:

- why you want the job
- the skills and qualities you have which will make you an excellent choice
- what you can offer the employer.

3

> The producers of a new television programme are looking for ten talented young people (aged 11–14) to take part. The lucky ten will be trained as actors, dancers or singers by the best in the business. They will live together for two months, working and playing hard as they polish their skills to be the best of the best and make it to The Big Time.
>
> To apply, please write to the producers at the address below, explaining why you're the kind of talent we're looking for.

Write the letter to the producers, persuading them to choose you to take part in the television programme.

Advise

These are the key features and skills of successful writing and, in particular, of writing to advise. You can find activities to develop these skills here.

Assessment focus	Key feature	Relevant pages	Learn how to:
1 Imagine	Plan	1.1 pages 6–9	plan and sequence your ideas
2 Purpose, audience and form	Answer the question	2.1 pages 34–38	read a writing task and identify the purpose, audience and form required
	Be aware of key features and appropriate register	2.2 pages 39–42	structure and shape your writing for specific purposes and audiences
	Select appropriate material	2.3 pages 43–47	select from a range of points depending on your audience
	Present your opinion using modals, imperatives and the first person	2.4 pages 48–52	give your opinion in a range of ways
3 Structure	Introduce and conclude your writing	3.1 pages 68–72	organise the structure of your writing
	Use connectives and linking phrases	3.3 pages 77–80	develop your use and range of connectives
		3.4 pages 81–84	use a variety of different methods to link your ideas and give your writing cohesion
4 Paragraphs	Paragraph	4.1 pages 88–91	organise your writing in paragraphs to support meaning and for effect
	Use point-evidence-explain paragraphs	4.2 pages 92–95	organise your points and ideas in effective paragraphs
	Connect sentences within paragraphs	4.3 pages 96–98	use pronouns and synonyms to give your paragraphs cohesion
5 Sentences	Use a range of sentence types and lengths	5.1 pages 102–105	vary sentence length and structure for effect
		5.2 pages 106–109	use a range of sentence types for variety and effect
	Rhetorical devices	5.3 pages 110–113	use a range of rhetorical devices at sentence level
	Select an appropriate register, usually standard English	5.4 pages 114–117	adapt the register of your writing depending on your audience
6 Punctuation	Punctuate correctly	6.1–6.5 pages 122–141	use a range of punctuation accurately

7 Vocabulary	Choose your vocabulary	7.1 pages 145–148	select the best words in your writing, thinking about their effect
	Rhetorical devices	7.2 pages 149–152	use a range of rhetorical devices at word level
	Check your work and develop vocabulary	7.4 pages 158–161	use a dictionary and thesaurus to improve the accuracy and breadth of your vocabulary choice
8 Spelling	Spell accurately	8.1–8.2 pages 165–172	improve and develop spelling strategies

QUESTIONS

A friend of yours recently applied to take part in a well-known reality television show. You have received this letter from them:

You know that show I auditioned for? I got in! I'm writing this letter from a secret address somewhere just outside London. I can't tell you where. I'm not allowed! Anyway, the reason I'm writing is this. Now I'm here, I'm not sure I want to be here.

I'm worried that I'll end up looking really stupid on television. Also, everyone here is much more interesting and talented than me – I'm bound to be the first one to get kicked out. And I'm really worried about the newspapers. You know what they're like. They always make up horrible stories about the people on these kinds of programmes and they won't leave you or your family alone. My mum's already had lots of newspapers phoning her up.

So what do you think I should do? Shall I tell them I want to leave? Or should I stay with it?

Write a letter to your friend, advising them what they should do.
You could write:

- advising your friend to stay (suggest how they could cope with the problems mentioned in the letter)
- advising your friend to leave (say why you feel the advantages would outweigh the disadvantages).

Every month, a well-known teenage magazine invites readers to be Auntie Agnes the 'agony aunt', giving advice and helping readers to solve their problems. This month it's your turn. Read this letter from a reader:

Dear Auntie Agnes

Every time one of my friends has a birthday, their parents buy them something really expensive. Computers, mountain bikes, games consoles, the latest mobile phone, the flashiest MP3 player, loads of money... they get whatever they ask for. The problem is that I feel really jealous because my parents cannot afford to buy me stuff like that.

My birthday is coming up in a few weeks and I don't know what to ask for. I would feel bad if I asked for something expensive because I know my parents haven't got enough money and I would be putting them under pressure to spend too much.

What should I do? Please help.

Yours desperately

Dan

Write your reply, advising Dan:

- what he should ask for as a birthday present
- what he should do about his feelings of jealousy.